A DEEPER FAITH

A DEEPER FAITH

A Journey into Spirituality

JEFF GOLLIHER

JEREMY P. TARCHER/PENGUIN

a member of Penguin Group (USA) Inc.

New York

JEREMY P. TARCHER/PENGUIN
Published by the Penguin Group
Penguin Group (USA) Inc., 375 Hudson Street, New York, New York 10014, USA •
Penguin Group (Canada), 90 Eglinton Avenue East, Suite 700, Toronto, Ontario M4P 2Y3, Canada
(a division of Pearson Canada Inc.) • Penguin Books Ltd, 80 Strand, London WC2R 0RL,
England • Penguin Ireland, 25 St Stephen's Green, Dublin 2, Ireland (a division of
Penguin Books Ltd) • Penguin Group (Australia), 250 Camberwell Road, Camberwell, Victoria 3124,
Australia (a division of Pearson Australia Group Pty Ltd) • Penguin Books India Pvt Ltd,
11 Community Centre, Panchsheel Park, New Delhi–110 017, India • Penguin Group (NZ),
67 Apollo Drive, Rosedale, North Shore 0632, New Zealand (a division of Pearson
New Zealand Ltd) • Penguin Books (South Africa) (Pty) Ltd, 24 Sturdee Avenue,
Rosebank, Johannesburg 2196, South Africa

Penguin Books Ltd, Registered Offices: 80 Strand, London WC2R 0RL, England

Bible quotations are from the New Revised Standard Version, except where noted otherwise.

Most Tarcher/Penguin books are available at special quantity discounts for bulk purchase for sales promo-
tions, premiums, fund-raising, and educational needs. Special books or book excerpts also can be created
to fit specific needs. For details, write Penguin Group (USA) Inc. Special Markets, 375 Hudson Street,
New York, NY 10014.

Library of Congress Cataloging-in-Publication Data

Golliher, Jeffrey
A deeper faith: a journey into spirituality / Jeff Golliher.
p.   cm.
ISBN 978-1-58542-404-7
1. Spiritual life—Christianity.   I. Title.
BV4501.3.G657   2008   2008025917
248.4—dc22

Printed in the United States of America
1   3   5   7   9   10   8   6   4   2

Book design by Meighan Cavanaugh

While the author has made every effort to provide accurate telephone numbers and Internet addresses at
the time of publication, neither the publisher nor the author assumes any responsibility for errors, or for
changes that occur after publication. Further, the publisher does not have any control over and does not
assume any responsibility for author or third-party websites or their content.

For Bob and Sally

CONTENTS

II. MAKING THE PASSAGE

The Season of Lent

Holy Week

The Season of Easter

III. THE PATH OF LOVE

The Season of Pentecost

PREFACE

There is a path—a spiritual path—that crosses the distance between us and God. That's what this book is about. We could debate whether the distance is great or small. We could gather evidence both for and against the existence of God, which has become customary. But all these arguments seem to fall flat somehow. It's the possibility of the path itself that calls out to something deep within my soul. I'm captivated by the fact that we—ordinary people like you and me—have the opportunity to catch even a glimpse of the Holy Mystery for ourselves. I realize that this seems fanciful, if not blatantly preposterous, to many people; yet I discovered that the spiritual path is real when I was nine. It changed my life then, and it still does. Since then, I've struggled with it, lost my way more than I would like to admit, explored it in different cultures and religions, and found a great deal of what I've been looking for. Now, some forty-plus years later, I try to help others who want to follow the spiritual path too. That's why I've written this book.

What you will find here is a collection of letters written to a friend who is struggling with life and God. The letters represent actual conversations that I've had with many people over the years—men and women, straight and gay, young and old, people of different religions, ethnic backgrounds, and cultures. They're written in the most open, candid, and uncensored way I know. The stories contained in them are true. With that in mind, I should tell you now that the path is not easy. I'm well aware of Jesus's famous saying "My yoke is easy, and my burden is light," (Matthew 11:30, NRSV), but this should not imply that following the path makes our problems disappear. I hear him offering encouragement. He's assuring us that the path is simple, even when life is terrible, and that *we can follow it* with perseverance and faith. The spiritual path teaches us how to live in a confusing and unjust world. It gives us the opportunity to live more lovingly, ethically, and creatively.

It helps us find unexpected answers where we believe none exists, and to see the Holy Mystery in places we would never expect.

Hugely significant issues of meaning and faith are involved. The kind of faith I know makes no claim to having all the answers about life and would consider it outrageously irresponsible to do so. I make no claim to understanding everything about the spiritual path. In fact, I'm not always sure how to live my own life. The day I make such a claim is the day I should leave my vocation as a priest, stop writing, and take a very long vacation. Faith is better understood as the leap we make into the unknown. The purpose of faith is to keep our minds open to the presence of God and our hearts filled with loving-kindness, precisely when "the answers" are what we don't have. For that reason, the purpose of this book is not to give answers, but to help us find our way. I understand this as being faithful to faith and to God.

There's no place for fanaticism on the spiritual path. Fanaticism is an overly simplified, simpleminded denial of life. Fanaticism is not simple. The spiritual path is simple. At the heart of the path, we find loving-kindness and an abiding respect for others and the larger body of life. We find a thirst for justice matched by a longing for forgiveness. Reason and common sense are necessary on the spiritual path—as expressions of faith—as is the willingness to think for ourselves, rather than joining in popular opinion. We certainly don't need more things to help us along the path. We have enough time, although we probably haven't realized that yet. There are no secrets regarding the spiritual path that we must find in order to follow it, or to establish its reliability and truth. To the extent that there are secrets, they involve history and the institutions that keep them. Those secrets don't matter very much. People who follow the spiritual path know that the most important secrets about life, religion, and God are the ones we hide from ourselves. Those secrets are quite real, and we find them as a result of following the path, rather than as a prelude or prerequisite that must be completed before we ever begin.

I realize that many people might take issue with some ideas found here, especially my deliberate use of these three words: "the spiritual path." Conservative-minded readers might assume that I'm talking only about the Christian path, which is certainly not my intent. More liberal-minded readers might say there are many paths to one God, which is true, while precluding any possibility of "the path" understood and followed from different points of view. To set the record straight, I am opposed to any effort at homogenizing religious traditions into one. Diversity is not only good, but intrinsic to life itself, as the eminent biologist E. O. Wilson wisely asserts. The same can be said for cultural and religious diversity. But we cannot lose sight of an even greater truth: namely, that people of all faiths who follow their own paths have a great deal in common. They know, from within their different points of view, that we're all brothers and sisters. They know that God is not the property of any one religion. This is not idealistic babble, nor does it dilute the integrity of different religions. Rather, it reminds us that the purpose of religion is not to divide, but to teach and exemplify a more loving, faithful, and respectful way to live. It also represents the faith and common sense that we're so close to losing in this turbulent time.

I should also say that I have no desire to proselytize, and I'm not telling anyone how to vote. I make no predictions about what the future will or should look like. Nor is this book about the relation between religion and politics, although the subject, which is as critical as it is thorny, comes up now and again as one subject among others. The spiritual path does not require anyone to look upon science as a threat or other faiths as something less, and it recognizes the all-too-obvious fact that people of all faiths, including you and me, are equally prone to making the same mistakes and forgetting the same essential truths.

Having said all that, let me make two suggestions about how you might read this book. First, it is organized around the ancient "holy seasons" of the church: Advent, Christmas, Epiphany, Lent, Holy Week, Easter, and Pentecost. These "seasons," which are based on the life of Jesus, represent the crucial stages and passages that followers of the spiritual path inevitably encounter. The fact that a book can be organized in this way already suggests that our lives can have purpose and direction, even within the confusion. However, this does not mean that the book must be read straight through, from beginning to end. You can begin anywhere you like—perhaps where you already are on the path, or believe you are. The letters themselves address questions, obstacles, passages, and leaps that we commonly face, and each one can be read entirely on its own.

The fact that the book can be read either straight through or by skipping around has significance for another reason. Life is not nearly as linear as we might like to think. It's not that God is capricious or unpredictable, but the path itself teaches that overly linear, step-by-step instructions can be misleading. Cookbook spirituality implies that if we do "this," then "that" will surely happen. Even worse, it suggests that we are the center of our own world. Anyone who has followed the spiritual path very long can tell you how doubtful these propositions are. Life is far richer and more complex than our self-serving representations of reality would have us believe, and the love of God actually does work in mysterious, unexpected, and sometimes miraculous ways.

Second, the book is meant to be practical. By emphasizing the word "practical," I'm not appealing to the part of us that asks, "What's in it for me?" This is not a path that encourages conformity to the way things are, especially the misleading sense of "me" as the center of things. One purpose of the spiritual path is to help us awaken to the wisdom we carry in our hearts, so we can weave it into our lives every day. In other words, the wisdom within us is revealed by the weaving we are willing to do—by the way we put our faith, knowledge, and common sense into practice. That is what I mean by "practical."

In the beginning, I was reluctant to write this book. I knew I would be discussing personal experiences that I normally keep to myself, and that seemed presumptuous. It could give the misleading and false impression that the book is about me rather than the spiritual path. But after discussing this problem on several occasions with my friends and editors, I gradually understood that personal experiences would be necessary in order to illustrate what it means to follow the spiritual path. Life is personal, which makes the spiritual path exceedingly personal. I just want you to know that this book is not meant to be about me. The more you read, the more you will understand exactly why I'm saying this.

Now, having finished my work and returned to the beginning to tell you what I've done, my opinion remains unchanged; it is presumptuous and maybe a little crazy to write a book like this. But it's even more presumptuous, not to mention reckless and perilous, to avoid our own experience, as if it doesn't matter. The world is fighting for oil, food and water, and faith; we are destroying God's green earth; but our times are troubled because we are. We need to recover a feel for the profound Mystery that life is. We need to understand our lives better as we actually live them. We need to be honest about who we are and who we would like to become. We need to be truthful in the way that love bears witness to the truth, and we need to be much less afraid. The spiritual path is about love, and eventually, love overcomes all the fear we harbor in our hearts.

Like I said, I don't know everything about the spiritual path, but I do know this: we always have the opportunity to live more faithfully and compassionately, and the vast majority of people I know want to do exactly that. If that's what you want, I hope this book will be helpful.

J. Golliher
Advent 2007

I

RESPONDING TO
THE CALL

The Season of Advent

1. CONFUSION

My Dear Friend,

Each and every day, when I walk down the long hill from my house to the mailbox, a magnificent apple tree catches my eye. I love that tree. I smile every time I see it. Yet, on this day, something better than that happened. I reached into the mailbox, found a letter from a dear friend, and the same smile came across my face a second time. I am so pleased to hear from you. How many years has it been? Twenty, thirty? No matter how I count, it's too many. Do you remember that last year before graduation? I'm sure you do—the fun, the worry, and some fond memories that are better left unspoken! So much has happened since the good ole days. I must say that your comment on my decision to be a priest is somehow comforting—that the news came as no surprise. A few others have said as much, including an aunt and uncle who felt sure that I was the last to know.

We can catch up later, if you wish. As I understand it, you've written to me as a trusted friend, who *happens to be* a minister in the church (I admit to smiling yet a third time). The way you put it reminds me of your ambivalence—and mine—about all forms of organized religion. Perhaps neither of us has changed very much in that regard. The fact is that I've always remembered you as a spiritually minded person, despite our feelings ways back when, and I wonder if you think of yourself in the same way now. It seems clear enough from your letter that something along those lines has been stirring in your soul for several months.

I'm more than happy to offer assistance in the best way I can, and my hope is that these initial suggestions will be helpful. First, let me say that I admire your honesty. Unnerving questions about life, pestering panic attacks, serious self-doubt—this is no picnic. Trust me. I know, firsthand, what you're going through, and my guess is that you never dreamed this would happen to you. My request is that you read my letter with an open mind. You believe your life has taken a turn for the worse—I believe your exact words were "a disaster in the making." But the situation, as I see it, may not be as bad as you believe. Nothing is wrong with you, at least no more or less than anyone else, and merely having doubts and disturbing questions does not indicate some strange or hidden personality flaw. Circumstances being what they are, you may think that I'm dismissing your concerns, playing down the significance of what you're telling me, or claiming that nothing is wrong while you "know" there is. Both views—yours and mine—may be entirely true. Taken together, they sketch the outline of a bigger picture, which is something you need at the moment. I hope you're willing to accept this possibility, that a big picture exists. If so, then you will begin to understand why I believe you're at the beginning of something profoundly good and deeply spiritual. My instincts tell me that you are willing; why else would you have written?

My second suggestion will be blunt. You have a journey to make, a sacred journey, that I hope you'll eventually come to understand as a path to follow. This will be the most important thing you've ever done. Call it the "call of God," call it the "call of the Spirit," call it the "call of the Great Mystery," call it a "catastrophe," call it whatever you like, but a "call" of some kind is hidden within the troubles. The purpose of this call may be to draw out something hidden and wonderful within you, and if you don't mind me saying so, to bring about your awakening from a kind of spiritual slumber. I should tell you now: the journey ahead may not follow a very straightforward path, with clear-cut steps to take and easily identifiable problems to solve. Why? Because the foundation of your life, the core of who you believe yourself to be, is shaking quite a bit. It doesn't really matter how secure or insecure you believe that foundation is. It is unnerving and outright scary when this happens. At the same time, all those doubts about yourself and questions about God are evidence of a Great Mystery at work within you.

Let me offer some practical advice too. The best thing you can do now is to create the space in your life that your soul needs. You need some time and privacy, which will give God and you the opportunity to sort things out together. Consider it a gift to yourself; you deserve it. I can almost hear you thinking, "My life is so busy already, I don't have time for this." People always say that. Don't believe it. The truth is that you've been knocked off your feet for reasons you don't understand. The sooner you accept this fact, the easier it will be to find the time and space you need.

I see no reason to panic, although the impulse to do so may be overwhelming and beyond your capacity to control. Yet the questions, the self-doubt, and the panic are neither the problem nor the enemy. In my view, they're your friends—good friends! Invite them to sit down with you and have a cup of tea. It might also be helpful to talk with flesh and blood friends and family about this; but if you do, remember that the real answers are ones you find for yourself. Reflect on your questions, all of them, while listening for their deeper source. It is precisely *at that source* that the Mystery, God, and the bigger picture are vying persistently for your attention; and, I might add, they have succeeded.

What alternatives do you have? You could try to forget all this. You could dismiss the possibility of a bigger picture out-of-hand. Those are two possible choices, but they both amount to choosing to sleep at the very time you're beginning to wake up. The choice is yours. Keep in mind that we always want to look for a reason, *the* reason, a specific cause, when something like this happens, as if we've done something wrong. You can also look for a chemical imbalance, if you wish, making it into an illness. In fact, it would be a good idea to see a doctor. At the same time, beware of interpreting your doubts and questions only as a temporary setback, like coming down with the flu or an overdrawn bank account in an otherwise "normal" life. It feels bad, and you want some medicine to ease the discomfort until it goes away! This would be the same as saying, "Forget about it."

I'm telling you this, in part, to help you through one of the obstacles found at the beginning of the spiritual path, and I want you to take the next step with as much confidence as possible. It would be a lie to say the way ahead will be a bed of roses. This is not a likely prospect. On the one hand, each step can seem very slippery at first; on the other hand, they will be no more slippery than life has always been—the significant difference being that your vision of life will become richer and more reliable. It's no surprise that "the God question"—again, these are your words—has surfaced at precisely this moment. This question, which is directly related to the doubts and confusion you are experiencing, is not going to be an easy one to answer. I want you to think deeply about the meaning of words like "God," "religion," and "church." You know from past experience that they can be loaded with unpleasant and negative meanings. This is true for many people—not just you. Those subtle (or not so subtle) memories are very important. Listen to them carefully. They might encourage you to close the very door that God wants you to walk through, and that is what I want you to avoid.

I want to be especially direct about one thing: "finding religion" is not always the same as "finding God." Our views and attitudes about the institution of the church depend on our background and experience. Quite honestly, the criticisms you have are entirely justified and true. My main concern, however, is "the God question," which is a very different matter. Its significance for you now depends on what or whom you believe God to be. I recommend praying, going to church, and being respectful of all things sacred. I love the church and struggle with it, but the better struggle is with God. Consider it likely that the ideas and impressions we've learned about God and carried around since childhood are not the whole story, and they may not be the source of the call that is shaking the foundations of your life now. It depends too on what you are looking for, and even more, on what God is calling out from your soul.

In addition to finding time for yourself, there is something else I might suggest. It involves paying attention to the people around you. Your friends and colleagues will have opinions, for better or worse. Listen with compassion, paying close attention, but without making judgments, as if you're meeting someone—both yourself and your friends—for the first time. Listen to the words and to the whole person speaking. As you learn to listen, you'll notice that most everyone will be right about some things and not so right, even wrong, about others. Some will say your doubts and questions are only symptoms of a "life change" that everyone faces at one time or another. In a sense, they will be right, and it could be good counsel. Still, what are they really saying, and what are you going to do with their point of view? Does it make your present situation seem different or any less important? Are they really thinking about you, or are they thinking about themselves? It could be both. Either way, is the gist of it true? *Is it really true?* Ask yourself what the truth might sound like from your soul's point of view. This may be a new and unfamiliar way of looking at your life, but it is entirely relevant to your situation now: What is being called out from your soul, from the deepest part of yourself?

Later, reflect even more on what you have seen and heard. You can do this anywhere and any time of the day or night—in the shower, at work, in bed, in the car, on the subway, in the kitchen, walking in the woods. By giving yourself space in this way, you'll cultivate a deeper sense of inwardness in your life. This inwardness, which is very different from self-absorption (as I said, the way can be slippery!), helps us appreciate the Mystery present within us and in everything that happens. I can guarantee that you need this much more than a new car, a new job, or new friends.

The spiritual path requires us to think for ourselves, perhaps in ways we have never associated with religion. Let me explain. People in our lives now and in the past fill our hearts and minds with memories of all kinds: events that happened years ago, last week, and today; disturbing things that people say, compliments, and simple joys. Anything that happens can shape our lives in countless, unexpected ways. All of these things come together in our minds to form perspectives about the way things are. These perspectives lead to decisions, which we make without really thinking or realizing what we're doing or how we really feel. This is one of the ways we "choose" to remain asleep in life. Everyone recognizes what this is like, but it's easily overlooked or dismissed as insignificant. "This is the way things are," we tell ourselves. What I'm saying is that *you must think for yourself and make your own decisions*—and this is why effort, privacy, and faith are necessary on the spiritual path. Again, my advice is to give yourself some time and space to sort things out. Get to know yourself again, without making judgments. Just observe, listen, and reflect. This will help you become aware of the Great Mystery that's been stirring up your soul so much.

My responsibility, as your spiritual friend, is not to tell you what the answers are (as if I could). No one but you can discover what God has in mind for your life. There is a God, but there is more than one way to find God, more than one way to make the journey, and more than one way to follow the spiritual path. As much as we might try, the Mystery is too immense to put in a box of any kind, whether large or small, or in any number of boxes. Still, "the God question" is staring you in the face. I hope you won't be put off by my quotation from scripture, but Saint Paul says something pertinent to your life at this very moment: "You know what time it is...it is now the moment for you to wake from sleep" (Romans 13:11 New Revised Standard Version).

The church remembers this same wake-up call every year in Advent, the holy season that marks the beginning of the spiritual path. We hear the call in scripture, through the voice of the ancient prophets. The Spirit speaks through them all, and the message can be heard anytime and by anyone, even you and me—usually in the guise of uncomfortable questions and doubt. These are echoes of our foundation shaking. It doesn't matter what our feelings and opinions about the church might be. It doesn't matter which religious tradition we follow—if any. The wake-up call is about God, our lives, and how we live them. Think about it. You're hearing this call now for a reason. I'm trying to tell you that the confusion is a sign of something good.

You can do this. Time and effort are needed, but we're not talking about "mission impossible." I have been through it, and I have faith in God and every confidence that your outcome will be good. I'll be thinking of you in the days ahead, especially when I see that apple tree in my front yard. Through all the seasons of the year, it keeps changing and growing. I smile every time I see it. It is a magnificent tree.

Faithfully yours.

2. DISCERNMENT

My Dear Friend,

I am truly pleased. There was always the chance that I'd never hear from you again. Instead, your thoughtful letter suggests to me that we're off to a good start. You're right to say that some changes in your life may lie ahead. Try not to imagine what they might be, not just yet. I would suggest, however, that your intuition may relate to some important ideas about yourself. The same can probably be said for some ideas about God. As for religion and the church, whether your opinions change or how they change is not of great concern to me, despite the fact that I'm a priest. I'm quite happy to answer any questions you may have, but there's no reason to worry about those things on my account. My thoughts turn only to you and the journey you're beginning to make.

It seems obvious that life may not be what you once believed. Let me make two suggestions. Like I said before, I want you to consider the possibility that your life is a spiritual journey. I'm talking about your whole life up until now, the present, and the future. Perhaps you haven't realized the truth of it yet, but eventually you will. We're all so distracted by other things, or we think of ourselves in other ways. But regardless of where our minds are, our lives have always been a spiritual journey of some kind. Talking with a priest doesn't change that; it doesn't make us more spiritual. Now—this is my second suggestion—you may need to prepare yourself to make some different decisions about how to live. Think of it like this: if your life is a spiritual journey already—and I believe it is—then the spiritual path that you're beginning will be how you live your life from this day forward. This, I believe, is where the greater portion of our time and attention should go.

Rather than being a problem, your feelings about religion actually bring to mind some fond memories of my father-in-law, Gordon, who was a real friend to me. I want to tell you a personal story I shared with him; but first, there's something you should know about Gordon as a person. Like you, Gordon would not have described himself as particularly religious. When the topic of religion came up, he listened, formed his own opinions, but never said very much. He didn't need to. His raised bushy eyebrows and the twinkle in his eyes said it all. It was the questions, rather than the answers, that revealed the Mystery of life to Gordon, and I loved him for it. His whole personality was organized around discernment—a traditional religious word, which I'm interpreting broadly. How do we distinguish between truth and falsehood, good and evil, reality and illusion—and delusion? To discern well, we must examine our own lives to a depth not usually believed possible or necessary. This involves listening to our instincts without jumping to conclusions, and it draws upon heart knowledge and intuition, as well as intellect. My point is that a discerning person is a faithful person, and discernment is necessary on the spiritual path. That's what the two of you have in common.

Unfortunately, Gordon is no longer with us, but I'm glad he spent the last year of his life with Asha and me. We lived in Manhattan at the time. He was frail, and our quarters were cramped. We got on each other's nerves from time to time, but I wouldn't trade that year for anything. It was not long before he died that I shared this story with him. I believe it helped him understand me. The story involves a childhood experience that I later understood as my discovery of the spiritual path. This is very different from saying "I discovered that churches exist" or that "religions exist." Gordon thought it was a good story. It turns on the issue of discernment, and the event that the story describes changed the course of my life, which is why I'm sharing it with you now.

One more thing: don't be distracted by the circumstances. I was nine years old at the time, living in the foothills of the Blue Ridge Mountains, where I was raised. I must admit that it seemed strangely comical to tell Gordon about this while we were sitting in our apartment on the thirtieth floor in midtown Manhattan. The Bible Belt and Manhattan seemed to have so little in common; and on top of that, Gordon was Jewish and I'm Christian. None of this mattered. We both understood that differences in age, place, cultural upbringing, and even religious belief   while they are important—take a backseat to something much more basic, thoroughly human, and deeply spiritual. But I'm getting ahead of myself. Here's the story.

It all began on the first day of a weeklong revival. The summer days were hot, and the revival was a special time to worship and socialize in the relative cool of the evening. Everyone knew everyone else's business in our small town, and I was sitting in a pew in the midst of them all. The church was overflowing with people, who were overflowing with joy. I could appreciate that, yet everything still seemed cramped and crowded. Even on a normal day, the "social" and the "religious" mixed together so seamlessly that any effort to distinguish between them would have been very difficult. At the revival, it was next to impossible.

The world would never be quite the same after that first night. The warm greetings, the spirited songs, and the Bible readings were all quickly forgotten. All that remained was confusion and fear— and my memory of the sermon. I was shocked by the idea that the world could be divided into "us" and "them"—the saved and the condemned, believers and unbelievers, or whomever one might construe "us" and "them" to be. I had probably heard this idea many times before, but I never paid much attention or believed it related to me. For whatever reason, I heard it now, very definitely, and I also noticed that everyone seemed to agree wholeheartedly with the minister. The worst part was the question it raised in my mind: Would I suffer the same fiery death as "them"—the sinners? His words painted a picture of a world that I didn't like; and as much as I tried to forget it, the dilemma he created in me could not be wished away.

For several days, I withdrew into myself, trying to make sense of what this new and disturbing world meant. My mom and dad were worried. I didn't realize that their views about God and religion were different from the minister's, and they weren't sure what was going on within me. Their good parental instincts told them that it involved the revival, but I still wouldn't talk. When my withdrawal persisted, they called a different minister, Preacher Morris, and asked him to come by the house for a visit. He was someone they respected as a sensitive person with common sense. Preacher

Morris agreed. He came to the house, and the two of us drove to the local cemetery to have a chat, privately. It was an excellent choice; cemeteries are quiet places, which makes them good for reflection and truth-telling.

After assuring me that my parents loved me very much, but were worried—I knew this already—the minister asked if I would tell him what was bothering me. I hesitated briefly, considering whether I might avoid an answer. I was afraid, and concerned about his possible reaction to my feelings. Somehow, I quickly found the courage, and I came out with it—"I don't understand why God punishes people." In fact, this was a statement of resistance on my part, not to Preacher Morris, but to the whole situation. But the fact that I told him the truth was a breakthrough nonetheless. I didn't like anything about the sermon, and I wondered about my friends at school who were not part of the congregation. What would happen to them? Would they be saved or punished? It didn't seem right, yet everyone in the church seemed terribly sure about "us" and "them." I, on the other hand, was no longer sure about anything: what it meant to have friends or how I was supposed to "be friends" with "them" now.

Preacher Morris thought for a few minutes; and as I waited, I saw kindness in his eyes. At the same time, I began to question whether my thoughts and feelings would bring God's punishment upon me. The conflict was terrible. My choice, in effect, was this: either join the church in order to save myself, while possibly losing those friends who might not be saved, or reject the church and lose my soul in hell. I told him what I was thinking.

He simply advised me to trust in God, to look into my heart, and decide for myself. That was the best and most "religious" thing he could have possibly said.

I felt compelled to return to the revival, despite my parents' concern and their assurance that I didn't have to go. I was reluctant and confused, but something drew me back. So, the following Sunday evening I did return, surrounded again by a cramped and crowded congregation. I sat quietly, thinking it over—piece by piece, question by question. The dilemma was horrible. It hung over me like a guillotine. I was embarrassed that someone would see the tears swelling up in my eyes, but I knew there was no escape from the choice that must be made: Would it be my heart and my friends, and the risk of burning in hell, or the more secure option of choosing the side of "us"? I began to wonder what being "saved" would mean if I decided to join the church, while secretly having my own private beliefs.

Suddenly, faster than I could think, I said no to any possibility of rejecting my friends at school. The decision was made. I sat there, alone, waiting for some kind of unknown, horrible punishment to drop down from heaven on my head. More happened within me in the next few moments than I can rationally explain. In one inward motion, instinctive and moral all at once, my soul was propelled by a force that I had not previously known. The fear and worries about myself and my friends lifted like a thick fog. The church was filled with holy light. I looked around shyly at the people in the congregation, wondering if others around me saw it too. Apparently they hadn't, but after a few seconds, it no longer mattered. I was awestruck and overjoyed by the light. I was free, and I knew it.

I was too young to have clear notions about "faith" or "God"; and yet the decision to follow my instincts was an act of faith. In fact, it was a leap *into* faith. I had no idea that I was making it, but I'm glad I did. Perhaps I haven't changed very much in this regard. I still believe—very definitely—that we must think for ourselves and follow our hearts. I believe we must be sensitive to the feelings and opinions of others, while remembering that sensitivity does not mean submission to social pressure. I don't believe the world is divided between "us" and "them"—the "saved" and the "sinners." Concerning the light, experiences like this are not necessary on the spiritual path; according to tradition, they can be a serious distraction. Nevertheless, they do sometimes happen to ordinary people, even to kids, and when this happened to me, it changed everything. I knew that God is love.

The last and most important part of my story is this. I don't recall much of anything about the fear-ridden minister. I can't remember what he looked like. I can't remember his name. But I remember Preacher Morris. He was a kind and decent man.

Faithfully yours.

3. THE WILDERNESS

My Dear Friend,

Your note may have been brief, but it certainly said a lot. You seem to be doing well *and* struggling at the same time. I'll ignore my better instincts and say it anyway—I know how you feel. In a certain mood, I might turn away if someone said that to me. It would probably sound obnoxious and patronizing: how could anyone else possibly know how *I feel*. So let me quickly add that I'm also struck by your sheer determination and desire. Only a few weeks ago, you took a big step simply by asking for help. How wonderful it would be if more people followed your example! And of those who take the first step, only a few actually go much farther, which is exactly what you have done. The words jumped off the page when I read them—"I really want to see this through." I couldn't be more pleased. Determination and desire are essential; yet, as I'll momentarily explain, you won't be able to plow ahead on the spiritual path, as if nothing more is involved. The purpose of my letter is to help you understand why I'm saying this; my hope is that you'll be able to hear it.

A good place to begin is with the nature and intent of my letters. I hope you always find them encouraging; but keep in mind that they're meant to be a mirror for you. When I share my personal experiences, my intent is for you to use them as you reflect on your life. You need to use this time to become more self-aware, without becoming self-absorbed. On the spiritual path, self-awareness is found through understanding, feeling, and foreseeing the consequences of our actions on others, not by looking into ourselves as if others have no consequence. I also want you to understand that my responsibility is not to tell you what to do, or think, or believe. I'm not asking you to agree with me; I'm not asking you to like or dislike what I'm saying or what you see within yourself; and I don't want you to give my words too much importance. Rather, I'm encouraging you to think for yourself; and as strange as it may sound, I'm asking you to realize that none of our thoughts—neither yours, nor mine—can define or contain who we really are. The spiritual path involves learning to see through whatever our egos want us to see. As painful as the process may be, and as much as we may resist it, self-awareness is inseparable from spiritual awakening. We don't seek it in order to feel better about ourselves, although that can be part of the path too. It's better to think of self-awareness as one part of the Holy Mystery that our whole lives are part of; and in perceiving this, we understand that even the smallest, seemingly insignificant, and broken parts of our lives are part of the Mystery too.

Why am I telling you this now? It's because of the ambivalence that I detect in your choice of words—"see this through." Don't misunderstand. You've done absolutely nothing wrong. I only want you to reflect on some assumptions behind the determination (which is still good) and the commitment that it implies (which is even better). My impression is that "seeing this through" really means getting through it as quickly as possible. Trust me—I can definitely appreciate how much you want to get on with your life. The whole situation is unpleasant, but, in all honesty, you should not expect a quick resolution. Even more to the point, there's something you need to find within yourself. Having been through *this* myself, my advice is to slow down. Caution is good, so slow down enough that your resolve and determination can be put to good use.

Try to remember that the spiritual path begins where we are *now*. This is the only place where a beginning can be made. Instead of trying to "see this through," let's give some thought to what "this" actually is. You won't find it on a map. You won't be able to see it with the naked eye, yet you're standing in the middle of it. I'm talking about a place that's well-known in all spiritual traditions. It has a distinct feel that you've already told me about in some detail: "a disaster in the making, confusion, a sense of being lost, life seeming to be out of control." "This," my friend, is called "the wilderness" or "the desert." The voice of John the Baptist, one of the great "wake-up" prophets, was heard as a "cry in the wilderness," which puts you in good company and makes your ambivalence perfectly appropriate.

To be in the wilderness is to face uncomfortable questions. Why is my life like this? Why am I so confused? What do I believe? Do I believe anything? Issues like these call our lives into question, and we usually react badly—which you, I might add, have not done (perhaps you haven't told me everything!). Usually, we put up strong defenses or tell ourselves that it's morally wrong even to ask these questions. But the purpose of the wilderness is self-awareness, and that's where I want you to apply your resolve. Don't try to "get through it." At least for now, the wilderness is where you are meant to be.

My advice is to slow down simply so you can listen. Give yourself the chance to hear what your heart says. Are the goals and direction of your life truly yours? Or do they reflect the wishes of others? You may resist. Maybe, somewhere down the road, you'll resist a great deal more. All this seems to be overwhelming and difficult. Maybe it is, but I'm being realistic, and believe me, I've been in the thick of it myself. The great irony is that we spend most of our lives in the wilderness without having much of a clue where we are—which is to be truly lost. For some, the church may be the wilderness; for others, it may be work or personal relationships. This really doesn't matter. The point is that when we become aware of the wilderness in our lives, and open our hearts to the gifts it has to offer, then the Spirit is much easier to hear. This is why the wilderness is a good place to be, and it's why I want you to slow down and pay attention to your life as it actually is.

There is more. Just hear me out and keep looking into that holy mirror of yours. In all likelihood, you believe you're being punished. "The confusion, the wilderness," we tell ourselves, "must be God's penalty for something that I've done wrong." So far, you seem to be willing to accept this, which is your way of believing that God is real. I can see the "logic" of it. It helps to explain the inner turmoil. I know you feel bad about yourself, and my guess is that you believe this so-called punishment is deserved. If secret wrongdoings exist, then by all means, we should discuss them. In the meantime, my hope is that you realize how judgmental some of these feelings actually are, even a severe judgment, rather than a statement of fact.

We do suffer the consequences of our actions; but the judgment I sense in your words is yours alone; it is certainly not mine, and I feel certain that God has a more generous view. I, for one, do not believe that God actually inflicts punishment. No doubt, some significant changes are taking place in your life. Have you considered the possibility that they may be good? Why jump to the conclusion that something must be wrong with you? Your caution is good, so be cautious about making unnecessary and premature judgments. This is what I mean by going too fast. Otherwise, you'll apply your resolve with great determination—in order to "see this through"— and end up running in circles. Slow down. The Spirit will help you through the confusion in God's own time.

The heart of it can be found in the difference between how God feels about us and how we feel about ourselves. I know how treacherous this territory can be. Vulnerable places in the soul are involved, places where we store tender, ambiguous feelings. I would bet that you feel unworthy, and the mere idea of "the spiritual path" probably seems presumptuous. If so, I hope you will remember one basic teaching: everyone, in some sense, is unworthy before God. Yet, we're unworthy *and* worthy. I know it seems contradictory, but both are true. Mainly, I want you to remember that "unworthy" does not mean "worthless." I know for a fact that they're incredibly easy to confuse, which has no doubt happened, and I pray you will not be so stubborn in your beliefs. You, my friend, are not a worthless person. That is not the reason you're in the wilderness.

I want to tell you a story about feeling worthless and its fiendish companion, shame. Think of them as unscrupulous people who sneak into our lives in the disguise of morality and truth. I met them for the first time when I was a youngster. I was with my mom and dad, browsing the aisles of a small general store, while they were shopping. I saw a small lock and key, which I wanted, so I put them in my pocket and took them home. I was too young to have a well-formed idea about theft, but I can remember my impulsive decision to take without asking. When my mom and dad discovered what I had done, they were angry and disturbed. They let me know how they felt in a clear and direct way, and the lock and key were quickly returned. Looking back, I would say that my parents taught me the lessons I needed to learn in a very healthy way. The result was that I understood perfectly well what I had done wrong.

The fact that I was guilty and ashamed of my behavior was not, in itself, the problem. The real experience of "wilderness" came with the feelings about myself afterward. What I'm describing is a struggle within the soul, a conversation of sorts, that we some-times find in the wilderness. This is basically how it went. At first, the feelings of shame and worthlessness entered my life as strangely comforting friends. I felt horrible about what I had done, and they gave the impression of moral competence and authority. I thought that I wanted "them" in my life. I thought they "should" be there and I "deserved" their presence. So, I invited them in, at least for a while. I let them have what they wanted: my attention and respect. In truth, I feared them and their judgment, but I assumed that I had no other choice. Here is the crucial part: I made a deal with my feel-ings of worthlessness and shame. I believed they were "right," and I would somehow receive their love and protection. I believed that I would regain my self-esteem and be held in high regard by all. All I had to do was believe in them, and they would conceal the sorry state of my soul from others.

For nearly two weeks, my life was utter misery. I remember walking along the road, by the post office, while my mom was shopping, thinking how much I hated who I had become. I knew deep down that I was not a worthless person, and I wanted my life back, regardless of my bad behavior. Yet I had struck a deal within myself that made me hostage to a false promise, based ultimately on fear. Unless I did something about this, the consequences would extend far into the future and well beyond the significance of anything I had done. Somehow I knew that every time I looked within myself, I would see my unwelcome guests. I would lose the freedom to think for myself, because my thoughts would be theirs. My ability to love other people would be distorted for years to come. I would live in constant fear—the fear of being seen as a damaged, morally crippled, worthless person. Unless I did something, I would wrap this same fear around my image of God. In effect, I would believe that God's way of being present is to cripple our sick souls, and then ask for our love in return. Unless I did something, I would believe in a lie, and I finally realized that I wanted no part of it.

What I did was this: I said an emphatic no to their presence— "No, I do not believe in you." I said it from the bottom of my heart, with as much inner authority as I could muster. It was that simple really. That is exactly what I did, and so can you. It took some time. I had to repeat those words over and over, but my unwelcome guests finally did leave; and now I'm telling you that you can do the same. Do you realize that you have the same inner authority? Have you ever tried to use it? Everyone has it; everyone can use it; but not everyone believes it. You don't have to accept that kind of world or that kind of God. My advice is to send those unwelcome guests packing as soon as possible. Otherwise, you may overlook the real meaning of your call, and miss the forgiveness, the joy, and the real hope that come within it. All you need to do is claim your inner authority and use it. The real, living God will set you free from the nonsense.

This is a terribly important point, so let me repeat it. These so-called friends—feeling worthless and ashamed—are capable of setting down deep roots in our lives, making themselves quite at home. When we let them, we end up thinking like them, even using their words, and giving them the authority to tell us how to see ourselves and God. It's very likely that you will meet these demanding, unwelcome guests in the wilderness. If so, do not feel sorry for yourself. You're only giving them what they want. To feel guilty about a wrong we have done in life is entirely appropriate and healthy, but to let shame become a part of our lives is a different matter altogether.

My counsel is simply to slow down. You are, in fact, in the wilderness, and you have an important task to accomplish, which is to reflect on your life. What do you really believe? What is God really like? Perhaps you might also consider the question that Saint Paul put to the early Christians in Rome: "Who will separate us from the love of Christ? Will hardship, or distress, or persecution, or famine, or nakedness, or peril, or sword?"—or, I respectfully add, your own demanding so-called friends? As for Paul's answer: "For I am convinced that neither death, nor life, nor angels, nor rulers, nor things present, nor things to come, nor powers, nor height, nor depth, nor anything else in all creation will be able to separate us from the love of God in Christ Jesus our Lord" (Romans 8:35, NRSV).

This will take some time. Going too fast is a sign of spiritual slumber—hiding behind our busyness, running away from something important, making hasty judgments about nearly everything, remaining oblivious to the very truths that the Spirit wants us to find. So don't expect an overnight discovery. On the other hand, I would expect the unexpected. In the mind of God, "one day is like a thousand years, and a thousand years are like one day" (2 Peter 3:8, NRSV). Look into the mirror, and let the larger vision emerge in God's time. The wilderness will give you every opportunity you need; and on the spiritual path, this is a very good place to be.

Faithfully yours.

4. The Adversary

My Dear Friend,

I would like to think that you really are taking time to sort things out, even getting some rest now and again. Have you realized yet that it's okay to be good to yourself? I like to take a walk early in the morning. The only requirement is that I go outside and put one foot in front of the other. Who would guess that a spiritual practice could be so simple? Give it a try. The light upon my face at sunrise is prayerful, even in the cold. It's the same with a spring rain. I feel so alive. I can remember a time, not many years ago, when I lost sight of those walks. Looking back now, I realize how distracted and pre-occupied I was. I had become my own worst enemy; and in the process, I forgot something I hope never to lose again. The purpose of my letter is to suggest how you might regain your life from the worst adversary you're ever likely to meet—I'm talking about you, but not only you. I'm referring to the adversary that lives within us all. It's such a contradiction: our worst adversary is also a great friend—and it's time to bring that person out into the open. But I'm getting ahead of myself.

I'm serious about those morning walks. They raise an important question: When inner peace has been lost and life seems to be falling apart, would taking those walks be of any real help? Or, as our inner adversary usually says, would it be an empty exercise, the burdensome motions of a meaningless ritual? I say it helps a great deal. Let me put it this way: do you remember the feel of the breeze on your face and the joy it brings? I expect your answer is yes, but is your memory working too hard, reaching back much too far? I believe today would be a very good day to go outside, take a slow, deep breath, and put one foot in front of the other. It really is that simple.

I know this must sound ridiculous. Here I am, recommending a peaceful morning walk, while you're telling me that you're in deep water, praying for God to send a rescue party. I can picture God's helping hand, pulling you from the depths, but I must say that this is better as a wish than it would be in real life. If your wish were granted, would you find the meaning you've lost? Would it be a transforming moment, or would it simply restore your life to the way things were before? Would it provide the answer to your questions about God? I don't want to seem insensitive, but a real answer is what you need. Your soul cries out for it more than you know; and to find it, you may have to live with the vulnerability and confusion—in the deep water—for a while longer. The temptation, which everyone faces, is to believe the journey can be postponed until tomorrow or the next day, when life is better and our troubles have passed. Yet God is with us in everything that happens, in the everyday things we do, in our successes, failures, and disappointments, in good times and over-our-head times. God is with you now, my friend, even in the deep. You have not been abandoned.

I'm suggesting that your rescue mission arrived some time ago, and I'm not talking about me. From where I sit, it's clear that you're beginning to see things differently. I hear you saying that you've made a crucial discovery—there is, in fact, more to life than your way of living has taken into account. Perhaps the deep water has been with you all along too. You've seen it many times, without realizing what it means, but now you do. This is exactly how spiritual awakenings begin. So much of what we see and recognize as the truth about life is shaped by the small part of experience that our lives occupy. And what happens when more of reality emerges into view? At first, we're disoriented and confused. We cry out for help. The irony is that we want to be saved *from* the very rescue party that has already arrived. Can you see it? I think so. In fact, you "see" much more than you did only a few weeks ago, which tells me that your heart and mind are opening. Life and God have brought you to this critical moment. It is a nerve-wracking situation, this is true, but all the crucial ingredients of a true spiritual awakening are there, waiting for you to put them all together.

You are a good person, making a difficult passage in your life. With determination and faith, you will find the answers you seek. Try to understand that your feelings are not yours alone. This admittedly difficult time in your life is not only about you. We're all in over our heads, and we're beginning to awaken to the truth of it. Think of your brother and his drinking problems, or your neighbors who can't pay their bills, and everyone's credit cards. Most of the world has no idea where their next meal will come from. For God's sake—we're altering the chemistry of the earth's climate, the atmosphere, the oceans, the deserts, the forests, the water. This kind of "falling apart" is what the prophets proclaimed centuries ago, and now you have the opportunity to see it for yourself. Let's face it, some part of us has always known that there's more to life than buying things, getting ahead of everyone else, and so on. This "knowing" may be denied, but somewhere within ourselves we know—we've always known. There have been times when I've heard you say it. The words seem awkward. They come out of the blue, maybe whispered silently under your breath, only to be shoved quickly away and forgotten. As uncomfortable and vulnerable as you may feel, what you need to do now is to pay attention. Better yet—listen. Listen to the world around you. Other people really do matter. Listen to Mother Nature. Listen to the crickets and the wind. Listen to the Spirit. We find ourselves in deep water because we would rather hear the sound of our own words. Hear the wake-up call again and again, however long it may take.

Having said that, I would not want to play down the deep water. My counsel is to do two things that might seem contradictory. Think of it as learning how to swim by letting yourself relax, or learning to think for yourself, while listening to other people at the same time. On the one hand, I am asking you to take those early morning walks. Remember the simple joys of life, and find some new ones. On the other hand, those walks are no escape. The water is deep, and the struggle to live, which is quite real, should neither be denied nor ignored. This really is about survival, and you must ask yourself what "living" and "surviving" really mean. Look at the world: fundamentalism and fanaticism, self-righteousness and finger-pointing; economic, political, religious wars fought in the name of good and evil. Each side blames the other. I would argue that if you choose any of those options for yourself, then you will be choosing sleep, or worse. You could drown in it, and take your friends, family, and everyone else with you. It may offer a semblance of direction and purpose. It may look like a rescue party, but where is the faith? The deep water is one way that God calls our bluff; and when this happens, the ego scrambles frantically to maintain its self-appointed place at the head of the table. This is when the name-calling and finger-pointing step in. This is when we become our own worst enemy. Make every effort to avoid it. Ask for forgiveness when you find yourself overcome by it. The struggle to survive is less about us and our egos, and much more about God. No doubt, this is difficult to perceive when we're over our heads and afraid, but it's the way of the spiritual path and considerably better than going back to sleep.

How do we stay awake? As a practical matter, I would avoid blaming other people and the world for your problems, and keep in mind that the "enemy" is, at best, an ambiguous notion on the spiritual path. When your mind becomes filled with such thoughts, remember that Jesus said we must love our enemies. The real "enemy"—our true adversary if there ever was one—would convince us to set aside Jesus' teaching. This "enemy" speaks inside our hearts; and sometimes, we give it an outward voice: "I can't do this," "I have no other choice," "Why bother?" "God has abandoned me," "I'm a failure in life." Take your pick. It's all half-truths and lies, but incredibly easy to believe. Much of the spiritual path involves learning how to recognize this amazing act of self-deception. It's a fact that we've all failed in many things. But this does not mean we are failures in the eyes of God. When you hear yourself say, "I am incapable of doing this," then know that your words are only half true. The greater truth is that we can't do anything without God, and with God, we can. The greater truth is that the most forbidding adversary lies within our hearts, and that is where the struggle for the soul is really found.

The adversary within loves to create and play upon our fear and the possibility of despair. Meet your half-truths, accusations, and false judgments with equanimity, while seeking forgiveness for those mistakes that are truly yours. The adversary would give us "the whole truth" in a nice, tidy package, which we might accept, forgetting that only God knows the whole truth about anything. I believe in God, but I also believe that God does not ask us to be right all the time. It's entirely possible to be right about one thing or another, even about the great religious and moral issues, and to show little or no love. I know you want to get things right, but I assure you that love is the way out of the confusion. If you can open your heart to this possibility, even for a moment, then the adversary will know that the end is near. The battle may rage on for a while. It may seem to get worse, but do not give up. Love will carry you home.

Let me close with this: when the tempting words of the adversary fill your mind, go for a good, long walk. Ask God for help. Very soon, a smile will appear on your face, and you will see the world very differently. Relax, despite the deep water. Do this as an act of faith—a leap into faith. Be determined, but patient. Show loving-kindness to everyone, including yourself. Awakenings rarely, if ever, happen all at once. There will be times when you will fail and want to give up. There will be fits and starts, and starting over. This time of year, the prayers of the church ask God to "give us grace to cast away the works of darkness, and put on the armor of light." Think of "armor" as the soul filled with God's radiance. This is the way to strengthen yourself and overcome the adversary within. Put it on like a new set of clothes. Put it on, even if it doesn't seem to fit very well. It's the same as forcing yourself to go on those morning walks when it feels like going through the motions. We're all in over our heads, my friend; and we must all learn to love and live again. I'll be thinking of you in the morning, as the sun begins to rise.

Faithfully yours.

The Season of Christmas

5. REMEMBERING

My Dear Friend,

Thank you so much for the beautiful card and note. The news of love reawakening in your life is the best Christmas blessing I can imagine. I realize how wonderful *and* difficult this time is; and I understand your complicated questions: What was I doing all those years? How could I have forgotten the love? How could I not have known? Those words, dear one, say it all. Because they come from your heart, they are the Spirit speaking within you. Don't look to me for your answers. Look within yourself and pray to God. Maybe you've been wrapped up in yourself and your worries. Maybe you've been working too hard. Maybe the ordinary burdens of life piled up and overwhelmed your common sense. All these are real possibilities. I'm not always sure that any answers exist, but I do know that breakthroughs on the spiritual path are often experienced in exactly this way—as remembrance and homecoming. I'm not talking about nostalgia for the way things were. Rather, a veil begins to lift; the confusion passes away; we remember who we are. The feeling is of a gift received long ago, which, for whatever reason, we overlook or neglect, and its meaning is lost. We catch glimpses of it sometimes. But these brief moments happen so quickly that we fail to see them;

and when we do, we tell ourselves that it's a fantasy or a dream. The miracle is that we can receive this gift again. This time, you know that it's real.

I'm struck by the combination of joy and melancholy, the touch of grief, in your note, and I wonder if you realize what this means. I hope my letter might help you perceive the meaning behind it. As strange as it seems, grief often accompanies holy love breaking through in our lives. Do not be disturbed by this, and don't try to avoid it, assuming that something must be wrong. This kind of grief is very good. It's a gift from the Spirit. Its purpose is to cleanse the soul—to make room for an even greater love yet to come.

Several years ago, I had a dream about this love and grief. Its presence and energy lives within me to this day. I remember new parts of it, now and again, or different parts, and glimpse whole realms of meaning I had not seen before. Sometimes I think the dream is dreaming me, or that the Spirit is trying to tell me something through the dream. Who can really be sure of these things? Nonetheless, it weaves together grief and love in a way that always nourishes my life and guides me along the spiritual path. I want to share this dream with you in the same way, as a gift, so I'll tell it as a story—with you as the dreamer.

Imagine a large lake. You're walking along its edge, reflecting on your life and enjoying the beauty of the day. You look across the water and notice how big the lake is. You can't see the opposite side, but you do see something strange floating in the distance. At first, it seems too far and too small to see clearly. Gradually, you recognize what it is: a beautiful, old wooden ship, the kind with large sails used hundreds of years ago. You look closer and realize that although the ship is burning, the water is calm, which seems peculiar. You see people on board, panic-stricken, crying out for help. You feel the difference between the two—the calm of the water and their screams—as opposing sensations within your body. Soon, you see massive flames erupting from the wooden deck and masts. Some people are searching for a way out. Others are waiting to be rescued. A few climb into small, crowded life rafts. You swim out into the lake, trying to help, but the ship is too far away. So, you return to shore, grief-stricken by the tragedy unfolding before your eyes.

Standing there, watching, you realize that the whole scene has another meaning. The ship, the flames, and the passengers represent you. They signify the sum total of your desires and fears: the desire for love, for power and influence; the fear of illness and death; the desire to help others, to do well in life, to be seen, to hide, to have more life— the fear that there won't be enough. You feel all this within yourself. You feel the flames of the ship burning in your soul.

Quickly, your gaze turns to the shore ahead. You walk in that direction and see someone—a holy person, a sage or saint—reclining on the grassy plain ahead. You step closer, and discover that it's Jesus, serene and Buddha-like. Or could it be Rama, the holy warrior at rest? You're not sure. You wonder who it is, but then your questions dissolve into the calm of the water present in *his* eyes. You see tears gently rolling down his face, yet his smile pours out the deepest kindness and love. You are drawn to him, but for a moment you stop, asking yourself why he's not doing something to help the people on the burning ship. Then you realize that he is. You are the ship, and he's helping you. You begin to merge with him. His heart becomes yours. You feel yourself becoming empty inside—free of illusions about yourself and the world. You're letting go of what might have been. You're letting go of trying to be someone else. Within the emptiness, you become restful and your heart is filled with nothing but faith. The same sorrowful tears in his eyes are present in yours, and the same love. This is homecoming, and you know it.

Sometimes dreams come from a place beyond the story they tell, and this is one of them, which makes me reluctant to say much more. I will say that I've learned a great deal from this dream. It teaches me that life is supposed to be overwhelming. To live in the presence of God is to be consumed by life. In any given moment, it doesn't really matter whether we're overcome by grief or love—or both. Our lives, just as we live them, are our spiritual journey. So, don't be afraid of living. Don't be afraid to be who you are. Do not be afraid to enter into the love *and* the grief.

The dream helps me receive the gift of holy love. If we bother to look, we can see it in each other every day. The soul's deepest longing speaks through the eyes. The question is whether in seeing, we will remember the gift, and take the time to receive it. The purpose of the spiritual path is to help us do exactly that. Be patient. With time, your heart will reveal the meaning you seek, and it will greet you like an old friend.

As you reflect on this dream, I want you to remember your past few months—sorting things out, persevering through the turmoil and confusion, and now, reawakening to the love you had forgotten. It's been an exceptional time. You could have denied the wake-up call and turned away. You could have denied the wilderness, and run away. Instead, you were faithful to the path. You have done all this, and the Spirit has bestowed its blessing—the grief *and* the love.

This, my beloved friend, is the nature of loving-kindness. God is not asking you to be someone else. God is asking you to be kind. The ancient prophets taught that loving-kindness, *hesed*, is the very nature of God. I hope you will place it at the center of your life. Let the light it gives be your guide. Share it in abundance with your family and friends. They are a part of your journey too, just as you are part of theirs.

On this holy night, Christmas Eve, we remember Christ's birth, the light of the world present in the here and now, in you and me, in everything and everyone that exists. I do not know the answer to your questions: "How could I have forgotten? How could I not have known?" Perhaps the answers are not very important, but I do know that your remembering is a sign of your homecoming. God spoke to Isaiah about this: "I am about to create new heavens and a new earth; the former things shall not be remembered or come to mind. But be glad and rejoice forever in what I am creating" (Isaiah 65:17–18). In this very moment, I'm reminded of the Christmas story. For Mary and Joseph, life was completely overwhelming. All seemed lost and there was no room in the inn. Yet they did their best with what they had, and it was enough. That is all that God asks of us, and this is what you have done. It was enough two thousand years ago; it is enough now; and it changes everything.

Faithfully yours.

6. Giving and Receiving

My Dear Friend,

You're exactly right—there's a big difference between the "holydays" and the "holidays." Christmas was commercialized well beyond the point of simple repair long, long ago. Oh well. Concerning how you might dig yourself out from under the "stuff," my advice may not be what you expect. Perhaps you're being a bit overly responsible about all this. It seems to me that Christmas celebrates the birth of a child, and acting our age all the time does little to make us more loving and joyful. Instead, I would suggest being like a child yourself. Most of the children I know are losing their childhoods much too soon, and I would like to think you might recover a large part of yours. You might also consider it to be a good example you can set for them.

Speaking for myself, I have fond memories of Christmas— the hymns and carols, the images of the wise men bearing gifts, the baby Jesus. I read somewhere that a child can be emotionally scarred for life upon discovering that Santa Claus doesn't live at the North Pole, deliver Christmas gifts, and so on. Apparently, it made no deep or lasting impression on me. I liked the story, but I don't think I really cared where the gifts came from. Like yours, the

Christmases of my childhood revolved around giving and receiving presents—mainly receiving. I suppose this makes Christmas seem entirely me-oriented and selfish. The spiritual adage is obviously right when it says that giving is more blessed than receiving. It is through giving—without counting what we may get in return—that we receive God's holy gifts. Nevertheless, I wouldn't overlook the deep spiritual significance of receiving. Receiving is part of the Holy Mystery too.

I'm serious about this. As a child, I rarely slept a wink on Christmas Eve. What a great feeling! Can you remember the last time you stayed awake all night with such joyful expectation? The season of Christmas proclaims a great gift, and this alone poses the question: How can it be received? The answer given by the Christian tradition is not that we *should* be more responsible, but that we *must* become like children.

The first real lesson I learned about receiving gifts was from a boy in my hometown. I was six or seven, and he was a little older. As the crow flies, our homes were only a few hundred yards apart, which wasn't very far in those days. I knew only a few things about him. For one, he was an avid walker. I knew this because I often saw him, barefoot, along the small road by the factory where he lived and most everyone worked. Also, I knew he was noticeably thin, and he had trouble speaking. I don't recall that he ever said a word to me, nor I to him, except a few "hellos" when we passed. If I knew his name, and I may have, I've forgotten it now. Our lives moved on parallel tracks, so our paths never crossed—except once.

It was his birthday. I knew this because the church arranged for my family to deliver his birthday cake—white cake with chocolate icing, one of my mother's specialties. It was a gift from the church.

My mother drove my sister and me along the small dirt road leading up the hill to his house. We found it and pulled off the road, looking for his parents, who must have been away. It was a small but lively house. Several children, brothers and sisters, I assumed, and a few dogs were playing in the yard. Most everyone in our town was poor in different degrees, but rich in the soul. Judging by the outward appearance of what I saw, his family must have been struggling more than most.

My mom carried the cake toward the house, meeting the boy just inside the gate. She handed it to him and explained that it was a gift for his birthday. I could see his eyes light up before she spoke. Joy burst from his face without the slightest hesitation. No self-consciousness. No overdone surprise. Nothing but pure joy. I don't recall ever witnessing such an outpouring of happiness. Our eyes met only for an instant. It was incredible. The light in his face seemed to move toward me, penetrating to a place within my soul. The force of it was so startling that I was shaken and teary. He took the cake in his hands, saying nothing with words, but everything through his eyes, and ran with it toward the house.

Along the way, the cake slipped from his hands. The entire thing fell to the ground. The car filled with stunned silence. I watched, waiting to see what would happen. To my surprise, he deftly scooped up the cake, a handful at a time, again without one trace of hesitation or the slightest change in demeanor. As if nothing had happened, he proceeded as quickly as before to the kitchen table, which we could see through their open door. There, he enjoyed his birthday feast with great satisfaction, together with his many brothers and sisters.

This was a confusing scene for me. My mind raced between

thoughts of what I had seen and questions about how I should be feeling. I remember wondering why my mother would have given my favorite cake to another boy. I felt guilty about thinking this, and then the sadness and shock returned with the disturbing image of the half-broken lump on the ground. Even this was confusing. I wondered if I *should* feel sad and disturbed, since he was so obviously overflowing with joy. As the difference between his experience and mine became painfully real to me, I felt alone in a way I had never known. I looked to my mother, wondering what she was thinking, and thought to myself that maybe I was feeling "grown up."

We sat in the car for a few minutes, stunned by what we had seen. I felt isolated, cut off from the boy and everything around me, which seemed dreadful and wrong—morally wrong. But then, a different kind of awareness rose up in me. A spiritual presence encompassed all my ambiguous feelings and thoughts. I felt close to the boy and shared the joy, which no longer seemed to be "his," as I had first perceived it. Now it was "ours" because he had given his joy to me. The bond I felt with him was sacred and strong, yet I knew how fragile it was. I felt teary again. I understood that my life was tied to other people, including those I didn't know. All that we do and say, our joy and pain, our prayers—all these have meaning. Our lives are sacred. We are heard and seen. We are part of everything that happens, and everything that happens is a part of us. We are witnesses to life and we are participants, and how we respond is witnessed. God knows us from the inside out.

Think of the boy—his spontaneity, his openness to receiving, his joy. He saw the gift, knew he wanted it, reached out his hands, and received it. If someone were to hand us the Spirit as a gift, would we receive it so easily? Or would we stand there, frozen in self-consciousness, waiting for permission, and wondering if it was real? If that child could find such joy in a simple birthday cake, then just imagine what can happen with you in your search for God.

Think of me, sitting in the car. At first, I was trapped by my own confused and conflicted feelings. Of course I was growing in self-awareness and empathy, and developing a sense of morality; but for a few moments, I didn't know what I should feel or what I wanted, and I was imprisoned by it. Is this what it means to be "grown up"— to be trapped within our own self-consciousness? Trapped so much that we forget how to receive the simple joy of life?

Now think of the two of us together, two young children, giving and receiving. From a grown-up point of view, I suppose it was sad that the cake was damaged, but it didn't matter to him. He just picked it up and moved right along to his birthday feast. Nothing on earth could have stopped him. That young boy taught me a great lesson about the spiritual path: our lives can be messy, confusing, and entirely unexpected, but each and every moment contains the possibility of true joy waiting to be given *and* received. He gave his gift to me simply by the joy in his eyes. The spiritual path can be that simple—and just as irresistible. Be like a child, my friend. Set a good example for your family and friends.

Faithfully yours.

The Season of the Epiphany

7. REST

My Dear Friend,

Only three days ago, I returned from a long-awaited family pilgrimage to Ireland. Six of us went, all packed together in a small van. Every minute was wonderful. You might not believe this, but I thought of you often, especially in Glencolmcille, a small coastal village in County Donegal. Saint Columcille (or "Columba") found rest and refuge there, fifteen centuries ago, but even now, anyone can see why he chose it. His time, of course, was very different from ours. Most of the Celtic monasteries fell into ruins years ago; yet many of the ancient spiritual practices live on, including the relationship known as "spiritual friends" or "soul friends." They took this quite seriously, helped each other through trials and hardships, and spoke about their search for God as if it was immediate and real. I believe it was. Reflecting on our friendship and the lives of many people I know, I like to think the difference between their experience and ours may not be so great.

I listened to your phone message with great interest upon my return, and I congratulate you on setting aside time for rest and refuge *after* the Christmas holidays. I'm not surprised that you need a break. I can also imagine any number of good reasons for it: ambiguous expectations, being alone when the company of others is what you need, or having excessive social demands when solitude would be the best of all blessings—not to mention the accumulated debt of holiday spending. Rest provides basic nourishment for the soul, and I'm glad you're getting some. But my concern here is not the need for rest. Those who follow the spiritual path also know that we can use rest in less than beneficial ways. This brings me to the real subject of my letter, which involves what you might be tempted to do with it, as there are many different kinds of rest.

Everything I heard you say suggests that you've reached an important place on the spiritual path. I'll return to your message momentarily; but for now, I'll only say that you've made a very difficult passage on the spiritual path, or nearly so. It's clear that the confusion and feeling of crisis have begun to fade, and you're finding solid ground again. My guess is that you haven't quite realized what this means. I want you to reflect on a few possibilities that I'm going to describe, and then draw your own conclusions about your present situation. Whatever conclusion you reach in your reflections, you have, in fact, reached a critical juncture.

The first kind of rest I should mention, *deep spiritual rest* or *resting in God,* is a holy gift. It arises from a deeply prayerful attitude toward life in every respect. To rest in God is an experience of relaxation like no other. Think of it as the body and mind slowing down enough for the whole person to relax. The dream I described in a recent letter, of the reclining Christ, points in that direction, but honestly, I wish I knew more. I want to know more. The implication of deep spiritual rest is communion with God while being in the world, a perfect balance of giving and receiving, action and spiritual mindfulness. Deep spiritual rest expresses the kind of faith that can be genuine receptivity to God's presence. I would warn against equating receptivity with passivity, which we're likely to do given the hectic pace of life we've grown so accustomed to. Those ancient Irish monks believed that going too fast (even in their time) was a great obstacle on the spiritual path, and their wisdom is timeless. While speed represents the epitome of action and alertness in our day, it really closes us off from the source of life. The purpose of the spiritual path is to put us back in contact with the source; deep spiritual rest is the outcome. Rather than assuming that this holy gift is out of your reach, which you're also likely to do, I hope you'll consider it as a possibility open to everyone, including yourself. Even a taste of it can change our lives. All we have to do is slow down, and put our trust—and ourselves—in God's hands. The Spirit will take care of the rest for us, so to speak.

Let's call the second kind of rest *doing nothing*. I would never devalue a hard day's work, but my experience is that very few people experience deep spiritual rest or "doing nothing." In practice, doing nothing is quite difficult; but its spiritual benefits can be astounding. I highly recommend it. Obviously I'm not encouraging you to shirk your duties and responsibilities. Instead, try doing nothing as an experiment in consciousness. In fact, I challenge you to set aside a whole day, a half day, even an hour or two, of doing exactly that—nothing. If you succeed, it will be a genuine achievement. I know that sounds a little crazy, but doing nothing from time to time helps us understand how busy our egos can be, even while the body seems to rest. We begin to appreciate how much our lives revolve around ourselves. That, more than anything else, is why we can be so resistant to any kind of rest, including deep spiritual rest. We tell ourselves we want it, but when the time comes we can always find something else to do. Doing nothing challenges the ego to give up its place at the center of our world; and behind that lies the fear that we really aren't the center.

The last kind of rest that I'll mention, *resting on our laurels*, is by far the most common of the three. By bringing it to your attention, I'm not insinuating that you're guilty of it, at least no more guilty than anyone else. When I visited Glencolmcille last week, I imagined that Saint Columba must have experienced them all, although I doubt he rested on his laurels very much. Maybe he did—a saint, after all, is still a person. Regardless, resting on our laurels is the exact opposite of deep spiritual rest. For anyone who follows the spiritual path, this ego-driven spin on the meaning of rest is an all too real and incredibly easy temptation to fall into. It's an attitude of the mind, which I'll sketch out the best I can. Perhaps the shoe doesn't fit your situation—I really don't know. You make the decision.

Without question, you've taken a huge step and made some significant changes in how you see things. Only a few weeks ago, you wanted to make room for God in your life; and now, as you put it, you need some *time away* for yourself. I can understand that, but I feel compelled to ask whether the prospect of God being present in your life seems a bit confining. Maybe it would put a cramp in your style. I can understand that too. What you really want, it seems to me, is a *rest stop*—some time away to find yourself again in the world you inhabit every day. By this I mean familiar landmarks that define who you are as a competent worker, as a friend, a parent, and so on. Your life has been shaken, and you want to feel self-assured and confident again, secure about your place in the world. I believe this is the kind of rest you want. Unfortunately, it presents a particularly difficult problem.

You may think I'm changing the subject, but bear with me. If the truth be told, it was your disgust with the "crass commercialism" of the Christmas season, together with your unexpected and rather quick comment on the "rightness" of "the church" that raised my eyebrows. In your message, you mentioned both in nearly the same sentence. I have to ask: Where did this sudden change in your view of the church come from? Apparently, you attended worship services during the holidays. I am pleased about that; but when you refer to "the church," I wonder what you really mean. Is it the church as a gathering of faithful people, or something else? I know as well as anyone that the church is a sacred institution *and* it is very human. It can have strong ties to other social and economic institutions, which makes it messy and morally ambiguous. What exactly are you talking about?

It seems to me that after all these years of rejecting "the church," you've just switched sides, and rather abruptly. Yesterday, you dismissed religion as morally bankrupt; today, you've dismissed the world for the same reason. Regarding the commercialism of Christmas, which epitomizes the problems of the world in your view, there's no doubt that it's overwhelming and gross, and it debases the sacred meaning of the holydays. Having said that, I want you to remember that many businesses would be lost without those sales, and a great number of people would suffer because of it. Somehow the bills and debts have to be paid. I'm not defending either "side"— the church or the secular world—nor am I denying that legitimate issues are at stake. I simply want you to reflect on the meaning of your words.

This happens all the time, especially at the beginning of the spiritual path. I'm raising the issue, hoping you'll realize that getting out of the deep water, which you have done, does not justify your jumping off the deep end. My primary concern is with you and the spiritual path, rather than the church and the invasion of the holydays by commercialism. What I hear you say is that you and the church are right, in a disturbingly triumphant sense, while the world out there no longer measures up to your new standards. Is that what you really mean? Is this the "new you"? Does finding some time for yourself mean resting on your laurels? I don't believe you ever intended to do this. I'm not even sure you are. But it certainly sounds like it to me.

My point is that "rest" is absolutely necessary on the spiritual path, and certain kinds of rest are actually a gift of God. At the same time, our uses of rest offer many subtle and deceptive temptations. For one, we might use it to crystallize worn-out thoughts and attitudes that, upon closer examination, we don't really believe. For example, your decision to go to church is wise, but I never suggested that you "change sides," whatever that means to you. Your newborn "righteousness" expresses the same cynicism you had before—it's only dressed up in new clothes. It may point in the opposite direction, suggesting that the direction of your life has changed, but it's still cynicism. To make matters worse, it's just as judgmental and presumptuous, perhaps even more so, and I can assure you that this is not the "armor of light" that will help you become free of the great adversary within.

It seems to me that you have found something incredibly important. Love really is awakening in your life, just as you told me only a few weeks ago. But then, having received this gift, you've begun to wrap it in some worn-out paper simply because it's available. Perhaps you picked up those ideas on television or even in church. Always remember the huge difference between deep spiritual rest—resting in God as an act of faith—and resting on your laurels. Jesus himself said that he had no place to lay his head, and when he took time for himself, I feel sure he was resting in God.

I want you to have confidence in the spiritual path, and I want you to be confident in your faith. But you need to think very carefully about the feeling of accomplishment that goes with it. I can guarantee that the gift you have received—the reawakening of love in your life—should not be seen as a personal achievement. I would look again in that holy mirror, and when you look, remember the adversary who lives within us all. The adversary loves cynicism. He uses it to make us smugly believe in our own "rightness"—until, by the grace of God, we finally wake up again. Instead of cynicism about the world, let me suggest that you make humility the measure of your faith.

Think of the wise men who followed a star in the East in search of the newborn Jesus. After they found him, they were warned in a dream not to return by King Herod, who wanted to destroy the child. The holy scriptures say they heeded this warning and "left for their own country by another road" (Matthew 2:12, NRSV). I suspect we would be much wiser to look at our lives and consider where this "triumphant" business will eventually lead. My suggestion is simply to get some rest for a few days by doing nothing. "First, do no harm"—that's what doctors are taught, and it seems entirely appropriate for anyone following the spiritual path. Who knows, you might find some rest in God along the way.

Faithfully yours.

8. Common Sense

My Dear Friend,

I hope you're in a better spirit than when we last talked. This is a difficult and awkward time, and the truth of it can't simply be wished away: you're having second thoughts about the spiritual path, serious ones, which I most assuredly understand. Now, sitting alone at my desk and wanting so much to offer help, I face the painful realization that whatever I write will somehow fall short. And yet, I remember times in my own life when the simplest words have made all the difference. I'm thinking of a warm "hello" from a dear friend after years apart, or the sound of my name gleefully shouted across a noisy and crowded room. In those moments, we hear and know that someone cares. It is the same with faith. When we feel lost or distressed, and our thoughts seem to scatter like leaves in the wind, God still gathers them up and hears them all.

Please tell me if I'm mistaken, but my impression is that you haven't said much to your family about your inner struggles, and only a few words, here and there, to a few close friends. I appreciate your concern about their possible reactions, once the truth is fully known. The fear is that they—all good and reasonable people who love you very much—will question your motives or common sense;

and now you're beginning to have the same doubts about yourself. Where, after all, will this lead? Who, in fact, will you become? Do you want to risk the loss of friends and the ridicule of colleagues? I can imagine Jesus saying "Follow me" to his disciples while they, standing before him, wonder if it will mean chasing a rainbow.

All your doubts, conflicts, and second thoughts are to be expected. What you really need at this moment is some confidence in a spiritual gift you have in great abundance: common sense. Your sensitivity to the feelings and opinions of others demonstrates how thoughtful and caring you actually are. In all honesty, if you didn't care about other people, I would be the one with second thoughts. While I understand your hesitation, I'm a little surprised that you've said so little to your family. I believe that the time has come, and I'm sure they will be interested. Just remember that the simple act of caring about other people is the best example of common sense I know. Keep your common sense and use it. Then, the worst kind of doubts and uncertainties about God will gradually resolve all by themselves.

I'm trying to tell you that common sense is part of faith. In practice, the spiritual path deepens faith *and* common sense. If the situation ever arrives that you're faced with such a choice, then remember this: either your common sense is in jeopardy or your faith has gone overboard. Under pressure, we might interpret them as entirely separate orders of existence, believing we must choose between the two. There are times when the spiritual path puts hard, maybe impossible decisions before us, but this is not one of those times. The Spirit is not asking you to choose between God and your practical nature or the respect of your family and friends, although I realize this worry lies behind the conflict you feel.

Instead of dwelling on your second thoughts, my advice is to put the energy behind them to a better use. You can rely on faith and use your common sense at the same time. First, let me suggest being practical about the experience of your family and friends. Maybe to them, the idea of the Spirit being a real, living presence seems foolish or intimidating. Surely you can understand their feelings. It's not easy for anyone to comprehend what believing in the Spirit means; I'm sure it's not easy for you, and honestly, I don't know anyone who really understands it. When you're speaking with them, it might be better to be more descriptive of your own life. Simply tell them about your actual feelings—even the confusion. Remember that they may have little firsthand knowledge of the situation you're actually facing. My experience is that almost everyone wants the assurance that our lives make sense and that a higher power will be there when we need help. For the most part, this means a God who will keep a reasonable distance—rather than call our lives into question—and provide comfort in our lives as they are. Despite these wants, it can be truly unsettling, if not totally disturbing, to experience the Spirit of God firsthand, or to want to, and this makes almost any conversation about it off-putting and easy to reject. It's no wonder you're having second thoughts. Even the most devoutly religious people, people who have followed the spiritual path for many years, can be uncomfortable and afraid. The holy scriptures say it straight out: "It is a terrible thing to fall into the hands of the living God" (Hebrews 10:31, NLT). If I were you, I would reflect on this as a practical matter, when you think about your family and friends. Empathize with them, rather than seeing any negative reaction on their part as an insurmountable obstacle or a reason to turn back.

Second, consider your situation apart from them. You're in the middle of a difficult passage, a trial of sorts, which, to be perfectly blunt, involves a much deeper inner transformation in your life than you might have guessed. You are growing spiritually, and the soul experiences growth pangs too. Christ put it plainly: "No one can see the kingdom of God unless he is born again" (John 3:3, NLT). Words like "born again" may not be easy for you to hear—not to mention for your family—and you have every reason to be wary. In this regard, it might ease your mind to realize that rebirth can take many forms, and it can be interpreted in different ways. Think of it as the passage from one form of existence to another—dying to a world that revolves around "me" while awakening to the realization that there is a God. And contrary to some well-deserved stereotypes, it is possible for people to be "born again" without closing their minds or becoming less tolerant. This is very likely the source of your anxiety and your family's concern. In fact, the experience of rebirth actually opens our minds and makes us more appreciative of the diversity of life in every respect.

It is sometimes necessary to leave familiar surroundings and the people we know and love, at least for a while, in order to make the passage. Perhaps this is another part of your worry. In your case, however, I would not even consider it. Actually, I would strongly advise against it. You're the one who is changing, my friend, and this will eventually deepen the relationships you already have. My suggestion is to overcome your fears, to listen to those closest to you, and if their fears are proven true—that you have become intolerant of them—then you and I have a great deal more to discuss.

I experienced essentially the same situation when I first told my friends in the university that I was becoming a priest. I was an anthropologist then, and I lost some friends when I made the transition. They questioned my motives and judgment. I also met some new antagonists in the church, who weren't particularly welcoming of an anthropologist, and they questioned my motives and judgment just as much. It was a difficult time, and I began to question my decision. Questions about evolution and creationism were behind much of the suspicion on both sides, but that was only the tip of the iceberg. Serious concerns about faith and freedom of thought were involved. None of it could be resolved by reason alone or faith. When all was said and done, and the transition was finally made, I found that most people in the university and the church are very much like me; they do not divide themselves into camps so easily. Deeply spiritual people can and do have very different points of view, but most everyone appreciates the Mystery that is life.

The real question I was left to consider was whether I understood what I was doing with a sound mind—that is, with common sense and faith. Neither the skeptic nor the saint (we can find both in the university and the church) has the last word about life and God. To believe otherwise is to stop following the path and to close the door to spiritual growth. If we are fortunate, we will keep the door open and receive glimpses of the Mystery. These insights and awakenings are holy gifts to be sure, but our understanding of them may change a great deal in the course of our lives. It is entirely possible to have more than one awakening, more than one rebirth, more than one transformation, and we still won't have all the answers.

My intent is not to downplay or dismiss the conflict you feel or your second thoughts. They are real, and your struggle with them is part of the passage. Perhaps you might pay close attention to Christ's own enigmatic words about this: "I came to bring fire to the earth....I have a baptism with which to be baptized....Do you think I have come to bring peace to the earth? No, I tell you, but rather division!" (Luke 12:49–51, NRSV). At first glance, this seems to contradict everything we know as loving, good, and holy. But look again at your divided thoughts, contentious feelings, conflicts within and without, and the estrangement you sometimes feel from others, including your friends and loved ones. Your inner conflict may be the sign of growing self-awareness. You're beginning to see what life has actually been like for a very long time. It's your awareness that is new—not the conflict.

Yet this does not mean that anything is wrong. In fact, something is very right—you're beginning to see and understand. The flame of holy love has ignited in your heart. This is the source of your longing, and its light makes the divisions *within your own heart* plain to see—your desires, loyalties, fears, and commitments, and your faith. Self-awareness always burns the ego. Your job now is to let the Spirit help you recognize the fears and insecurities for what they are. Self-awareness and spiritual awakening go hand in hand, just like common sense and faith. I've said this before: ultimately, the issue is not about being "right." The issue is not whether you are right and they are wrong, although I know it seems that way. The only thing that matters now is whether you choose to be loving. The whole universe revolves around that one question. You have received the invitation.

Now, let me add a few words of caution. I do not believe God creates conflict for the purpose of testing our faith. I do not want you to go looking for conflict in order to prove that God is present in your life. To do so would be to manufacture a self-fulfilling prophecy that only confirms itself. It would be the equivalent of saying "I told you so" to your own reflection in the mirror—one appearance speaks to another—while believing we hear the voice of divine inspiration. It's a cheap and deceptive way to put yourself at the center of attention. However, the fact that you're feeling this conflict, without creating it, is reason enough to be encouraged. What matters now is your response. You are being asked to use your common sense, to face up to the shadows, *and* to find the faith to walk through it with love. You are not being asked to choose between one and the other. But this is the trial, the ordeal, the passage that leads to rebirth.

So, a real turning point has come. Do you remember what you said a few weeks ago? "I really want to see this through." You can either back away from the anxiety in your life, or seize the moment as an opportunity. If, in God's time, a single moment can open to eternity, then what good does it do to reject other people—those who don't hold the same views as ours, who haven't had the same experiences, or who don't stand up to some standard we create in our own minds? In the passage of rebirth, common sense joins together with faith; forgiveness with love; grief with joy; and confusion with clarity. Our divisions are not so much overcome as transcended. All you have to do is follow the path of love. The Spirit will show you the way.

My advice is to talk with your family and friends, but mainly I hope you will listen. Care more about them as people rather than worrying about any second thoughts and doubts you carry around within yourself. Remember, the world does not revolve around the "me" we create in our minds. "We" describes the path much better than "me." Consider what you're actually going to say in their presence. Would you try to prove a point, as if "the God question" can be solved in a debate with winners and losers—as if faith can triumph over common sense, or common sense over faith. You might win; you might lose; but nothing would be resolved. Either way, that approach would show very little love, which means you would be leaving the spiritual path.

I know you feel isolated and alone; I know you have serious second thoughts; I know you're afraid. The truth is that you've done absolutely nothing wrong. This is what the spiritual path is like. The greater truth is that you can make this passage. When you do, it will be a step into love; and you will know that prayers are heard—like hearing the sound of your name spoken across a noisy and crowded room. Your heart will leap; your face will smile; and you, my friend, you will be exceedingly glad.

Faithfully yours.

9. A Leap into Faith

My Dear Friend,

I've pored over every part of our last conversation—the difficult family meeting, their unexpected question, your answer, and your dreadful resentment about feeling caught off guard and tested. I've sorted through it all, again and again. Now, as I finally prepare to write, there's nothing I would like more than to break through that hard shell of yours. I would, if I could, but only God and you can do what needs to be done. You, dear one, have made a hugely wrong turn on the spiritual path. My concern is that you seem so oblivious, and I know that if you stew in self-pity much longer, you might leave the path altogether. This could happen. My purpose in writing is to help you find it within yourself to face the truth. Do you dare try? I'm talking about making a true leap of faith, and I should tell you now—it will be a leap *into* faith. Whether you have the desire, the courage, and the good sense remains to be seen.

Do not let the relentless tone of my letter suggest anything other than the deep respect and, indeed, the love with which I am writing. For that reason, I am holding you accountable—not to me personally, but to the spiritual path. This is not about your family, but about

God and you. I must say it straight out: You have grossly misunderstood the meaning of your family discussion. I actually do agree with them, very much so, in fact. Their question—"What are you really looking for?"—is superb. You can resent it all you want, but this is exactly the right question, and they have every right to ask it. People are justifiably suspicious of religion these days (including you, I might add!) and your family only wants to know what the stirrings in your soul mean and where they might lead. Surely you can understand this. Besides, has it occurred to you that Jesus put this same question to his disciples? He did. Have you considered the possibility that the same Spirit is speaking through your family? I think you should. Questions, on the spiritual path, can be just as important as answers, perhaps even more so. Not only that, different versions of this one very good question have been echoing from them *and* me for several months. Now the Spirit has called it out into the open. And what have you done? You tell me that you dislike being tested. The only honest response I can give is simply this: "Get over it." Everyone is tested from time to time. Life is a test. Difficult situations arise; significant questions are asked; and we don't always do very well. Our egos are bruised. So? What you haven't understood is that you're being tested in a much larger way—not by your family, and certainly not by me, but by the Spirit. The great irony in this whole situation is that you believe you have failed (isn't this the real issue?) when, in fact, you have done exceedingly well.

You may not believe this, but I love your spoken-from-the-heart words—*I'm looking for God, and I don't know where it will lead*. I concede that it fails to address their immediate concerns. You feel embarrassed. But think about it. People usually assume that grown-ups have their lives all mapped out, with achievable goals and a clear sense of direction. Sometimes this is the case; sometimes not. In any event, you are not that person right now; and regardless of this, you have not failed anyone—not your family, not God, and not yourself. No one has questioned your personal integrity, although your resentment tells you otherwise. No judgment has been made about you, except the one you make about yourself. Until this point, at least, you have been honest with yourself about yourself. This is essential on the spiritual path. Even more, you said it out loud, which shows courage and integrity. By speaking so honestly and genuinely, you have come very close to a huge leap of faith. You've almost made it, and you still can. Now, all you have to do is let go of that miserable resentment and pursue the question. This may take some time and determination, but do it anyway. By all means, trust your honesty—and if you really believe that I've never been in a situation like this, then think again.

This is how it happened to me. I'm walking through an unfamiliar neighborhood, feeling a bit lost. I'm not surprised at feeling lost because I've recently moved, and I know very little about the town. Something has been stirring within me for several months, and that, combined with the move, crosses my mind when I see a church in the distance. I walk closer, thinking that it might be good to talk with a priest, but finding one you like is not always easy. I notice the church has a well-kept, welcoming appearance, so I go inside. Introductions are made: first Joan, the secretary, and then Peter, the priest, in his study. Their unpracticed smiles and compassionate looks tell me that I've found the right place. While glancing at his calendar to find a time to meet, Peter turns toward me, thoughtfully, and says, "By the way, is there a specific reason you want to see me?" As I heard it, this was the same question asked by your family—and Jesus. Peter could not have known that his simple question would cut so deep.

I would have loved to give an ordinary, honest answer—a carefully guarded secret, a confession to make, a known problem to solve. Some guilt about not attending church would have been especially good. But I have no answer to give, except "I don't know," which is what I say. His slightly raised eyebrow catches my attention, and I suspect that a favorable first impression has just been lost. If I had taken the time to think, I might have said more, making up some quick half-true answer on the spot. Later on, I would be glad this didn't happen. I might have believed my own words, or tried to believe them, and this would have set in motion a half-true conversation for our next meeting. His perfectly good question would have been avoided, as well as the greater truth behind it. As it is, I find myself talking with a priest without knowing exactly why and unable to explain myself.

Peter's gift is listening, and I soon realize what a tremendous gift he actually has. I need the opportunity to explore the question, which I do by talking about everything that comes to mind: my work, books I read, ethics, politics, and justice, worries and frustrations. That is how my leap of faith begins. I have no idea what I'm looking for, but I'm determined to find it, so I talk about everything. I find my first clue early on, about three weeks later, when I realize how difficult our one-way conversations are for Peter. I see his eyes glaze over, and I know why. It's easy to know. I've grown weary of hearing my own words—circling endlessly, round and round, like a model train on a very small track. If I feel this way about myself, then listening to me must be a real chore for him. This seemingly insignificant, but terribly humbling moment cracks the door in my heart just enough. We've been talking about important, weighty things, at least in the abstract, but the truth is that Peter is bored, and so am I. Not only has a stranger walked into his office for no apparent reason, but now he finds out that this stranger is boring. I wonder what, in God's name, he must be thinking of me. Throughout the many years of our subsequent friendship, he never says a word about it. I suppose not every truth in life needs to be spoken out loud.

Everything changes the following week. I'm embarrassed by our previous meeting. On my way to the church, I'm thinking that Peter either dreads our appointment or laughs about it, and I think about not going. I realize that this is my ego talking, and I begin to understand how wrapped up in myself I really am. What I don't know is how to unwrap. Once I arrive in his office, I sit in the same chair as always, drinking my coffee, eating my pride. He asks me how things are going. I begin talking, just like before. Then, in mid-sentence, the same self-recognizing awareness of the week before returns, only this time multiplied many times over. It carries a force that shakes my whole being. Suddenly, I enter a deep state of meditative prayer. No decision is made about this. It just happens, spontaneously. No words form in my mind—none whatsoever. I'm not talking to Peter. I'm not even talking to myself. There is utter silence not only in the room, but also within me.

I can't explain this in the usual rational terms, but I would not be exaggerating to say that the Spirit reached down and covered the part of the brain that produces words. In another sense, I experienced my own personal train wreck, which is how our answers sometimes come on the spiritual path. The collision happened when the Spirit raised my awareness enough for me to see myself. I was shaken by it, but freed from my own thoughts and preoccupations in life. Peter and I both feel a palpable presence of the Spirit in the room. Some time passes within the silence—I don't know how much. Then, I slowly gather myself and turn my attention again to him. Without taking even one moment to reflect, I say some of the most plainly honest words I have ever spoken—"This has all been nonsense." I am thinking of everything I have said during the previous weeks. All of it had been "true" and important; but in those silent moments, it had no significance whatsoever. My words are not a judgment, but a statement of fact. I am being truthful about myself to myself; and by saying it out loud, I'm telling Peter that my leap into faith has been made. My own hard shell has been cracked open, and my soul can breathe again.

I should also tell you that the conversation ended with another good question—"What are you going to do now?" All I could say was this: "I really don't know, but I will be back." It is the truth, which is enough. Perhaps, my friend, you might consider saying something along those lines to your family. A little reassurance couldn't hurt, and it's so much better than self-absorbing resentment. Lent is approaching too—forty days of self-examination, repentance, and forgiveness, which we all desperately need. Use this time well, by preparing for your leap *into* faith. Despite anything your ego may be saying, you have been honest with yourself and your family, and I am proud of you. Just imagine what might have happened. You might have said what you believed others wanted to hear, simply to impress and to please. You might have given the "right" religious answer to Jesus' question, even quoting from the church's teachings about who Jesus is, "The Messiah," while avoiding the question altogether. Instead, you told the truth. Jesus himself addressed this very issue: "Not everyone who says to me, 'Lord, Lord,' will enter the kingdom of heaven" (Matthew 7:21, NRSV). If your words confess that you don't have all the answers, or any answer, then I say, "Praise God." Keep searching. Basic honesty will steer you in the right direction.

Faithfully yours.

II

MAKING THE PASSAGE

The Season of Lent

10. ENDINGS

My Dear Friend,

Images of "the Fall" came to mind when I was walking through the woods this morning—Adam and Eve driven from the Garden. I would like to avoid any speculations about the meaning of this fascinating, controversial, but dreadful story, and the only reason I bring it up is that your letter provoked it. So you believe you've reached a dead end! You're telling me that a door, a gate, a passage on the spiritual path is permanently closed—at least to you. Setting aside any opinions about the opening chapters of Genesis, I think you're looking into a rather grim mirror, and I want you to be careful how you interpret what you believe you see. Surely the great body of life—heaven and earth—has not been designed to keep anyone out; however, I will admit that the world we live in every day suggests that it has. Gatekeepers do exist, and we've all met our share of selfish ones. Their only job seems to be to keep people out. My guess is that you've projected this pitiful, pitiless job onto God, and now believe the spiritual path has been closed to you. This is the grim mirror I'm talking about. I would like to remind you that Jesus is portrayed as a gatekeeper too, but of an entirely different kind. Not only that—he claimed to be the gate itself, and his aim is to help everyone make the passage.

I want you to pay close attention to what I'm telling you. Your instincts are good; and, in a manner of speaking, you are right—a dead end has been reached. This is entirely true, but that does not mean the passage has come to an end. I'm asking you to hold these two contradictory thoughts in your mind at the same time. Can you do this? Are you willing to try? I believe you can and you will. I only wonder how strongly you believe in dead ends. You may truly believe, as a matter of conviction, that doors in your life—particularly this door—will always remain closed. Maybe you want to believe in them for reasons locked away somewhere in your heart.

Let's assume that you're not really going to give up, that you're still willing to give it one more chance. If that is the case, then I'll make two suggestions. First, I want you to examine the nature of your belief, which, in my view, is really a deeply held *disbelief.* You tell yourself that a door will not open, and that's that. I say it will. We could argue about this forever, and it wouldn't matter in the least. Just look more closely at this disbelief within yourself. Are you really talking about a closed door? Or are you describing an image you have of yourself? Second, I'll suggest a deep form of prayer that I hope that you will make into a daily spiritual practice. I'll describe it in due course, but let me say now that you must be willing—and you must make a decision to follow through regardless of your feelings about it. It will *not* be necessary for your whole heart and mind to be entirely present. For now, I'm only asking you to put your body and words into it. Stay with it for a while, and your heart will follow.

Very soon, we will be entering the most holy time of the church, which represents the most difficult part of the passage. It begins with Ash Wednesday, the first day in the Season of Lent, when we turn our attention solely to self-examination and fasting in preparation for Holy Week. The teachings of the church say that anyone can make this passage, but no one can make it alone. The fact that you're beginning to realize that *you* really can't do this tells me your instincts are good, and precisely for that reason, all your doubts have surfaced—with a vengeance. Believe it or not, this is a perfectly normal reaction, given the circumstances. You actually are following the spiritual path, so don't be surprised that it's difficult. There is, in fact, more to life than we can accomplish on our own. We really do need God's help. And when our minds finally meet up with reality, our egos don't like it one bit. Welcome to the spiritual path.

Concerning your self-examination in Lent, I suggest reflecting on some burdensome expectations you've likely placed on yourself. You say that you're getting nowhere. You say a dead end has been reached. But what do you mean by "making progress" on the spiritual path? What do you really expect to find or feel—whether today, tomorrow, or the next day? Maybe we all expect to follow the path for a while, and then wake up one morning to find all our problems miraculously solved. That's what we expect: a world of pleasantly endless possibilities. As good as these images and expectations seem to be, they can be paralyzing. We fantasize about a world where so many choices exist that we make none. To pick and choose everything means that our hearts aren't dedicated to anything or anyone—except, perhaps, ourselves. We end up with nothing, accomplish little, and remain stuck in our own far-fetched expectations. Can you see it? When we finally realize that *our* expectations are not fulfilled, and aren't going to be, then we find ourselves in a world of frozen disbelief.

Be very wary, my friend, of any desire you may have for perpetual beginnings that never end. It's much better to consider the possibility that endings have an unavoidable but wonderful meaning. To avoid the endings in our lives is to become trapped within our fantasies, which is another form of disbelief—our running away from reality. As a result, we never really make the journey. We're always ready to begin, but never quite willing to follow through. The dead end that you've reached is your awareness of the fantasy that has come to an end, and I'm trying to tell you that endings are good. I'm asking you to have faith that endings are part of the Mystery too. Ash Wednesday represents the beginning of the end. It symbolizes the closed door in your life, the dead end. You are right—this ending is definitely real. But instead of turning away, you can follow the spiritual path by entering into the ending. Every person must do this alone, and your time has come.

My advice, at times like this, is to examine our feelings about the permanently closed door very carefully, and take them to God in our prayers. Honestly, what else are we going to do? Do we really want to give up now, believing that the door will remain forever shut? We might. To make matters worse, we might believe we're hopelessly lost and beyond help, or that the spiritual journey is one big illusion, a lie perpetuated by the church, and that the spiritual path itself is a product of human imagination. What else, we ask ourselves, could better explain the endless repetition of the same uncertainties and doubts after so many months and years?

Now is definitely the time to remember those personal qualities that have brought you to this place in your life: honesty, loving-kindness, perseverance, steadfastness, your genuine struggle with life

THE SEASON OF LENT

and faith. You have these qualities and you've used them well. They have kept you on the spiritual path. And you're right about something else. All these good qualities are not enough, not even close to enough. I do not deny all the disappointments in life, the wrong turns, the uncertainties, the feelings of getting nowhere, the dead ends, the closed doors. There is every rational reason to turn back. Yet, in the face of all this, we can still take the next difficult step by entering into the ending. We can do it as an act of faith. Spiritual traditions speak of hope when everything seems pointless, and they say that God never gives up on anyone. You are right about the dead end. Tradition is right about faith and hope. You're both right, and it's not easy.

So what now? I can't tell you exactly what to do, but I will share with you what I do. This is an ancient spiritual practice, deeply rooted in the Christian tradition, and based on one of Christ's teachings that I take quite literally. It begins with the tell-it-like-it-is words we hear on Ash Wednesday:

Remember you are dust, and to dust you shall return.

Although these words may seem startling and abrupt, they express one of the most clear-minded thoughts we will ever hear. The fact of our mortality is unavoidable and very real, and of all the endings in our lives, this, obviously, is the ultimate one. There's absolutely nothing morbid about this. To remember we are dust puts everything else about the here and now in perspective. It is the truth. There is an ending.

The next step is to follow Jesus' directions about how to pray. In a very simple and straightforward way, he says,

Whenever you pray, go into your room and shut the door and
pray to your Father who is in secret. (MATTHEW 6:6, NRSV)

I want you to find a quiet, secluded place, perhaps a room in your home. Go there, alone, and close the door behind you. You are the one closing this door—no one else, but you. Before you begin to pray, I want you to do something else. Never mind that it sounds a little crazy. Remember that image you have of the permanently closed door—the dead end? The door with a sign over it that says, "It's all pointless. I'll never get anywhere on the spiritual path." We give up or never try because we've been told so many times that the door won't open. Instead of turning away, I want you to face the truth about yourself. I want you to yell at that closed door in your mind. Do it as an act of defiant courage or as an act of faith, but do not take "no" for an answer. Yell at it until you're sick and tired of yelling. Yell at it until you find yourself laughing. Whatever it takes to break the spell, do it. This gate cannot be taken by storm. We can't knock it down, but we can overcome our disbelief. We can enter into the ending.

Finally, while you're still in your room, I want you to say the "Jesus Prayer"—the Prayer of the Heart—with as much devotion and loving-kindness as you can find within yourself. This short prayer comes from the Eastern Christian tradition. The words of the prayer, said repeatedly in a mantra-like way, are simply these:

Lord Jesus Christ, Son of God, have mercy on me, a sinner.

The words are ancient, and if you say them enough, the Spirit will carry you into the depth of your heart—and his. This is the actual "room" that Jesus is really talking about. The door will open, because Jesus will open it for you.

I should warn you now that the mind always resists. As negative thoughts arise—they inevitably will—simply observe them, without making judgments, and then return to the words of the prayer. Let them carry you, gradually, to the place of deep spiritual rest within yourself. Jesus will help you find it. I hope you will do this spiritual practice throughout the forty days of Lent—this is my suggestion. It will be a huge step on the spiritual path. Even if it makes no rational sense, I want you to do it anyway.

Obviously, the kind of Lenten fast I have in mind involves much more than giving up chocolate. I'm talking about shedding the belief, whether conscious or unconscious, that we have been abandoned, that we have no choice, that we are forever stuck in the way things are. This great passage of the spiritual path requires our "dying to the world." It is the ancient way. We are mortal creatures with immortal souls. Yet even death, our greatest fear, cannot prevent God from opening that door that seems so clearly shut. It is possible to enter into the ending we're so eager to deny. You are right—this is an ending—but the passage still exists. I'm encouraging you to enter into this ending as an act of faith, and I'm telling you that there's more going on in heaven and on earth than we know or believe.

Faithfully yours.

11. JUDGMENT

My Dear Friend,

Some time ago, you asked me to comment on a story in your local newspaper. According to the report, a congregation located not far from your home tried to banish a family from their church. Why? Because they supported the "wrong" candidate in the presidential election. Actually, I had read the same report in my paper here, and my reaction was much the same as yours: I was appalled; but even more, I was pleased by the family's response. Most people would've made a quick exit, probably holding back their feelings to avoid an unpleasant scene. This family, on the other hand, did the unexpected—they refused to leave. You have to admire their courage and their faith.

I must apologize for the long delay. My hope was to learn more of the facts before saying anything. As it turned out, no follow-up ever appeared, and I've been unable to discover the details for myself. Yet the time was well spent. I had the opportunity to reflect on why this story struck such a disturbing chord; the separation of church and state and the more general relation between religion and politics are two good reasons among others. For our purposes, it's unnecessary to know how the family voted or what the specific issue(s) behind the conflict might've been. My immediate concern and yours is judgment, which the congregation seems to have in great supply. Their behavior bothers you; the proximity of their church to your kids and school magnifies it. The whole incident has stirred up, once again, some personal questions about God's judgment: Is it real? Does it have any resemblance to the news story? And, more to the point, how will you be judged?

This covers a vast territory and an awful lot of judgment—their judgment of the family, your judgment of the congregation, and God's judgment of you, me, and everyone else. We've touched on this in previous letters, but now we should go a great deal deeper: first, by examining your reaction to the incident; and then, by considering how I, a parish priest, navigate the treacherous waters of politics and religion. I'll also share a story that is very different from the one we read in the paper—one that offers a glimpse of what God's judgment might be like in the here and now. I'll save that for the end. If my letter is a bit longer than usual, it's because the issue of judgment can be such a terrible stumbling block: we want to follow the spiritual path, but we resist the accountability.

My guess is that you feel trapped between two simultaneous influences on your life. Neither is very pleasant. Although they seem to be the same, the only thing they really have in common is the word "judgment," which may explain some of the confusion. The first influence involves your reaction to the news story. I'm glad it affected you personally, and I'm glad you were upset. Yet the congregation's attitude toward the family has increased your anxiety level more than it should, and that has thrown you off balance spiritually. Perhaps I'm wrong and I don't mean to chide or criticize, but I believe you've given them power that they don't really have: power over your emotions and your peace of mind. There's no doubt that they've crossed a line between politics and religion; and in doing so, they've also trespassed on your soul, despite the fact that you're not a member of their congregation. My concern is that you've consented to it. Clearly some crucial boundary issues are at stake here. You must guard yourself against influences of this kind on your life and you must be watchful about your susceptibility to them. It's never a good idea to give your soul to anyone, under any circumstance—except your family and God, and even then, I would be careful.

Second, your persistent concern about God's judgment suggests that a genuine response to the Spirit may also be at work. This should be taken seriously. It's not uncommon for people who follow the spiritual path to become more aware of God's judgment, rather than less. We all must face the consequences of our actions. I believe this is happening to you, but God's judgment is very different from the congregation's dreadful behavior toward that family. I've made more than my share of mistakes in my life, but I have no experience of God's judgment ever taking the form of branding or pushing away anyone, which is the exact opposite of the news story. God's love and forgiveness are infinitely greater than ours. Ultimately, that's what you need to know. To say anything more—about the "end-times," for instance, or "the Last Judgment"—would be simply repeating what I've occasionally read or speculating about matters that no one fully understands. Keep your eye on the ball. It's hard enough to live your life faithfully every day, without having to take into account ambiguous ideas about cosmic history too.

My advice is to begin disentangling these two influences—your reaction to the story and your worry about God's judgment—as soon as possible. Otherwise, your desire to follow the spiritual path will lead you in one direction, while your anxiety-ridden indignation will pull you in another. Put the brakes on worrying, and give yourself a lot of time to think this through. Questions like these are rarely, if ever, settled once and for all—at least until we meet God face-to-face. To prepare for that day, my advice is to reflect on Jesus' simple teaching: "Do not judge, so you may not be judged" (Matthew 7:1, NRSV). What do you think he means? That you shouldn't care about the church and politics? I doubt it. That anything goes, or that it doesn't matter what you think? I doubt that too. I believe he wants you to follow the spiritual path in a discerning, well-balanced way, using good judgment without being harshly judgmental about other people. Remember the spirit of his teaching: He's offering encouragement combined with compassionate, yet *uncompromising* guidance. He isn't being judgmental; he's just telling it like it is.

Now, let's take a closer look at the news story. For many people I know, incidents like this conjure up the worst stereotype about religion; namely, that it works in the name of God, but as an instrument of political (and economic) power that stigmatizes those who lie outside the fold. I know this sounds cynical and bleak, but there's some truth in it, and it is how you feel. If you weren't so polite, you would have said it yourself. I happen to agree with you, but agreeing with your friends doesn't say very much. It's better to think through the kind of response you might actually make in a world like this. Two immediate possibilities come to mind, both of which I hope you resist. You could reject the world, religion and politics included, but what would the outcome be? You would cut yourself off from a world that you are, in fact, part of and care about a great deal, and then end up talking to yourself, slowing suffocating your soul with a lot of nonsense. Or you could launch your own campaign against what you don't like, making it into your new religion. And where would that lead? In all likelihood, you would feel happily redeemed, yet an already bad situation would become considerably worse, and everyone else would slowly suffocate. Do you see my point? Just thinking about it makes me short of breath. The last thing you should want is to let some fanatics become a reason for you to reject anything, especially the spiritual path. Don't give them your soul, simply because you find their attitudes distasteful.

There is a third possibility. Think of the deeply faithful people—much like the family in the newspaper—who have stood up for their beliefs in the face of severe social pressure and crushing institutional power. Many have gone to prison, tragically and unjustly. Many more have lost their families and friends, their jobs, and their lives for the sake of God and the spiritual path. I'm not saying this could or should happen to you—I hope it doesn't—but I want you to remember that people really do follow the spiritual path with a great deal of integrity. They listen to their hearts, and they follow the Spirit. Remember them. Even if you don't know their names, they are your friends. Think about that. Perhaps you might consider calling that family in the news on the phone. They probably live somewhere in your neighborhood. I'll bet they would be thankful; they could probably use your support, and you might learn a great deal from them.

As for me, a parish priest, I'm deeply involved with all kinds of political issues—environmental and economic justice, human rights, and community development, to name a few—and I frequently discuss them from the pulpit. We can't be silent about the public issues that shape our lives, or pretend that hiding our heads in the sand is either desirable or right. Silence suggests a relationship of acquiescence to the way things are, if not outright approval. Yet—I cannot emphasize this enough—God and the world are not the same. I haven't asked you to tell me who you vote for; I don't tell people how I vote; and I never endorse candidates from the pulpit. When we enter a holy place, we need to know that everyone is welcome, equally, without distinction of any kind. We need to acknowledge that no one has all the answers, that we all make terrible mistakes, and that each and every person deserves hospitality and respect as citizens *and* as children of God. For that reason, it is dangerous, spiritually, to blur the difference between a political constituency and a gathering of the faithful. Even when the cause is entirely right, an invisible wall tends to go up with a sign saying, "Not everyone is welcome here." My responsibility is to encourage people to be involved in public life, while making sure that dreadful sign never goes up. Places of worship are holy precisely because they are God's—not ours. To claim them as our own is to stake out a territory that has never been ours and never will be. It's not only an act of trespassing, but also theft. As much as we might deny that we would do this, it happens all the time. The temptation is always there, because the darkness is there—within us.

That's why Jesus encouraged us to be in the world, but not of it. He was asking us to seek God first and to be loving, forgiving, morally responsible people in our lives every day. Perhaps this hasn't occurred to you, but people who follow this path generally become less judgmental in their opinions of others, rather than more. Why? Because we become more aware of God's judgment, rather than less. The love of God, which we seek, draws out the shadows *within us*, so they can be acknowledged and healed. We become less judgmental because those shadows, or the greater part of them, are made up of our own false judgments circling back on us. That's what we must face, rather than projecting it onto others. To tell ourselves that it's not there, or that it exists only in people who disagree with us, is both outrageously foolish and a clear indication of fear.

But there's no reason to be afraid. It's the unacknowledged shadowy side of ourselves—and even the darkness (I'll say more about this at another time)—that should make us concerned. For the most part, we become aware of it simply by trying to live faithfully every day. This is perfectly normal and natural. There's nothing somber about it. This kind of awareness helps us to lead a spiritually balanced life by reminding us of the utter hypocrisy behind our judgments of other people. If anything, it's a good reason to give thanks; and, from time to time, it brings a good laugh at ourselves. And there can also be times when the light seems to reach down into our souls and pull out large handfuls of nasty sludge. When this happens, we *can* learn our lessons and move on to the light that's been calling us all along. Trust me on this: it does happen, it's not easy, and the outcome is the healing of the soul.

Now I want to share a story about God's judgment. I have two reasons for choosing this particular one: first, it might help you understand how our longing for God's love can make us more aware of God's judgment; and second, the story involves trees. It seems to me that if the church seems a little claustrophobic to you right now, then you should go outside and find an especially large oak or grove of oaks and breathe the fresh air. As you'll see, this is reason enough for the story. But whether you pray indoors or out, the truth about ourselves is unavoidable on the spiritual path.

I love trees. I'm well aware that some segments of the church have not always approved of this, and God knows that I don't worship trees. Nevertheless, trees are sacred, and I'll tell you why. They breathe. They take in carbon dioxide, while giving us the oxygen we need. Their breath makes ours possible. Without them, we wouldn't exist. They hold vast amounts of water aboveground. Although we don't see it, it's there: in their trunks, branches, and leaves. Water is sacred too. I baptize people in the same water that once flowed through the body of a tree—and the bodies of many trees—just as it will again. And let's not forget some famous biblical trees: the tree of life, the tree of knowledge of good and evil, the cedars of Lebanon, the oaks of Mamre, and, of course, the tree that bore Christ's crucified body. Like I said, trees are sacred.

Anyone who has walked through a grove of live oaks knows what I mean. Their long, mossy, interwoven branches form a magnificent canopy that has a striking resemblance to the vaulting structure of gothic cathedrals. Years ago, when I lived in south Louisiana, I often sought them out as refuge from the searing heat and humidity. But I love to be near trees, all trees, for another reason too: they help me feel close to God. My awareness changes when I walk under their branches. The part of my "normal" thinking that objectifies and depersonalizes people or any part of the world simply falls away. When you experience the world in this way, there's no question about helping anyone in need. You just do it. And it's not that you naively or childishly love everyone and everything. You just stop worrying about it, and you become more aware and more open to the truth about the way things are. If you remain there long enough, you see the sunlight radiate in all directions. You know that light is a sign of God's love, and you're a part of it. The idea of being judgmental about anyone seems foreign and wrong, and when thoughts like that rise up in your mind, as sometimes happens, they feel hostile. The world becomes an object again, and so do you.

That's what happened on the day I want to tell you about. I was walking beneath the canopy for maybe thirty minutes. The play of light and shadow through the towering branches above was wonderful. I remember thinking how beautiful it was, when suddenly my attention turned to the shadows stretching along the ground. They seemed unusually heavy, so much so that the mere sight of them was disturbing. Gradually they took on the appearance of hard substance. Gazing at the shadows interrupted the feeling of being part of the world around me. I became aware of myself in a different way, and I didn't like what I was seeing—in myself. I felt that I was being seen and known. But by whom? Was it the trees? Was it me looking into the mirror of the trees? Or was it God watching me look into the mirror? In the moment, it didn't matter very much. All I knew was that a power greater than me was aware of everything that was happening; and somehow, that same power was helping.

To gather myself, I took refuge at the foot of an especially large oak. One after another, I relived scenes from the past. I had done plenty of things that I wasn't proud of, and I remembered plenty of them, but on that day my mind was filled with memories of hurtful, unfeeling comments that I had made to friends, and some smaller but exceedingly poor decisions that affected other people in ways I deeply regretted. After thinking about it for a while, all the details merged into one large and terrible waste that I was making of my life. That was the truth of it. The energy, the gifts, the opportunities, the Spirit—all misdirected and misused on who knows what. Once I faced it, I understood that the darkness had to be brought into the open. I had to confront the part of myself that believes I am so right, when, in fact, I am entirely mistaken. I sat there and cried until I was tired of crying.

I put the cross I was wearing around my neck into the palm of my hand. I had bought it at a nearby abbey only a few days before, where it had been carved and blessed by the monks who lived there. I stared at the cross, and imagined Jesus crucified from the branches above. I prayed that he would save me from the judgment I was feeling. Suddenly, I could see myself praying. What I actually saw was a person feeling sorry for himself, and I knew that God was completely aware of my inner condition. I looked strange to myself, as if it wasn't me, or it wasn't the person I wanted to be. In that moment, I realized that God doesn't go around looking for our failings and shortcomings. God wasn't singling me out. God only wants us to stop putting up those dreadful unwelcome signs, to stop pushing people away, and to stop putting Jesus back on the cross. I wondered what was I really asking Jesus to save me from. To pray for God's help in times of real need is one thing; but to ask God to deliver us from our own healing is totally absurd—in effect, that's exactly what we do. The darkness within us is the last thing we want to see, but eventually the spiritual path leads us directly to it. God's judgment is both unavoidable and real. As horrible as that sounds, there is nothing that anyone should want more. Rather than running away, we can embrace God's judgment like the homecoming it is meant to be. By acknowledging the darkness within and seeking God's forgiveness, we are forgiven. This is the miraculous, redemptive, totally undeserved form that the love of God takes in our lives. I took a deep breath, waited for a few seconds, and then stood up on my own two feet. It seemed like the right thing to do.

When I look back on that day, I always remember the trees. They taught me that the whole of creation participates in our healing. There's no one to exclude because everyone and everything is involved. And now, I'm reminded of the family in the news story. They found themselves in the middle of a thick darkness, and they stood up too. They stood up for what they believe to be right. My guess is that they've passed through the darkness before, or they will very soon. Either way, they're telling their congregation—and you—that there's a different kind of path to follow and that there's no reason to be afraid. Why don't you pick up the phone and give them a call?

Faithfully yours.

12. THE SELF

My Dear Friend,

I've been under the weather for several days, fighting a cold or the flu. It's been frustrating. My energy returns in the mornings, but by the afternoon I feel drained and dispirited again—which, of course, is the reason my letter has been delayed. Nevertheless, this irritating bug has been valuable. It's given me the time to rest and reflect that I've needed, but would not have taken. Among other things, I've been thinking about these letters and my half of our friendship. I'll bet you would be surprised to know that I've never been a good correspondent. It's true. Over the years, my friends have been quick to chastise me about this, and rightly so. The neglect I've sometimes shown in this regard has been a serious failing in my life. When I think, as I often do, of some dear friends who died much too young, my regret becomes especially painful. There's so much I wish I had said, and so many stories I would like to have heard.

Behind this failing has been a sometimes stubborn reluctance to say much about my inner life. A number of wise people have tried to help me work through this. They've told me straight out that I shouldn't keep to myself so much, but, until recently, I haven't listened. No—I heard them. I just didn't take it seriously. I remember well an older counselor who once said, "Jeff, you're not a selfish person, but you take your privacy issue way too far, and it could be seen as selfish—maybe it is selfish." He understood that privacy was my way of protecting myself from a hostile world, not that the world really is hostile or that I need protection. I rationalized this for so long that I elevated my overdone privacy to the level of moral virtue, confusing it with self-effacing humility. Once he said it, I knew he had put his finger on the truth. It can take a long time and considerable effort to see such things within ourselves. We must want to see it, and it helps to listen to our friends.

For that reason, my letters are written not only for you, but also for me. They've become a spiritual practice of sorts. I don't see them as penance—that is to say, my payment for a spiritual debt I owe—although I suppose this could play a part in the larger picture of my life. In any event, I write them willingly and with a great deal of gladness and joy. They give me an opportunity to express some things that I've kept locked away, and this helps me understand the person I have struggled to become, for better or worse, and what I have learned. My only regret is that I have not done this sooner. I suppose it doesn't matter very much now. When all is said and done, my real hope is that you will find my letters helpful and encouraging.

You've asked a good question: "Can too much self-examination make me self-absorbed?" The answer is definitely yes, and the fact that you're aware of the possibility tells me that your self-examination in Lent is going quite well. On the one hand, self-awareness is absolutely necessary on the spiritual path. On the other hand, you need to understand that while self-awareness and spiritual awakening are inseparable, they are not the same. I'll do my best to address your question by making a few general comments and laying out some principles that have been useful to me. But I do hesitate. Ultimately, you're asking whether the spiritual path helps us to realize the self or to overcome it. The only answer I can confidently give is simply to say both, depending on what you mean by "the self." What I know for sure is that you can get lost in it; and without a basic framework, this is territory that can be terribly difficult to navigate.

Until now, I've been reluctant to discuss "the self," simply because I've wanted to avoid a heady, overly abstract discussion about it. I do hope you'll read what different religious traditions, philosophers, and psychologists have to say. Study is good. Knowledge is good. Discussions about the ego, the higher self, lower self, and all kinds of selves in between can be helpful. Many people, for instance, have argued that the self may not even exist in the ultimate sense you seem to have in mind—which is entirely the point: the "self" we know exists largely in our minds. I'm not asking you to believe in any particular view of the self—Western, Eastern, psychological, theological, hermeneutic, and so on. *I just want you to realize that reading about the spiritual path is very different from actually following it.* Nothing compares with direct experience. To experience something firsthand radically transforms who we consider ourselves to be, and when that happens, we realize just how much we have been hiding behind what we think we know.

My advice is meant to be practical. Whether the self really exists or what it means are subjects we could debate, but people who have followed the spiritual path for a long time still have an "I" that speaks and describes what they experience. This is the *person* I'm concerned about—the ordinary sense of "I" and the never-ending "my" and "mine" that we all know. I like to think in terms of persons. And I want you to remember that, as individual persons, our capacity for self-deception is so pervasive that it probably characterizes human existence as a whole. My counselor's insight is a good example: I had confused my desire for privacy, which he saw as potentially selfish, with the virtue of humility. Perhaps "self-centered" would be a better word for this, but I was deceiving myself in any event. The difference between "selfish" and "self-centered" may be quite useful to you, especially during Lent, although any overly drawn distinction between them suggests the kind of outlandish maneuvering the ego can do to defend itself. My point is that we can devote a great portion of our lives to doing unselfish things—like helping other people—while being almost entirely self-centered at the same time. Does this mean we should refrain from helping others until we overcome our own personal issues? Of course not. To do so would amount to utter selfishness and indicate the kind of self-absorption that you're concerned about.

Having said that, my advice is to turn your attention toward *basic garden-variety self-centeredness*. Self-centeredness permeates our lives in ways that can be very difficult to perceive. This relates to why Saint Paul, with such honesty, could say, "I do not understand my actions. For I do the very thing I hate. . . . For I know that nothing good dwells within me, that is, within my flesh" (Romans 7:15b, 18a, NSRV). Yet, he also proclaims, "I have been crucified with Christ, and it is no longer I who live, but it is Christ who lives in me" (Galatians 2:19–20, NRSV). My guess is that you may struggle with this. Many people struggle with it, including me. It seems to negate the reality of our best human instincts as well as the goodness of our common humanity. Yet it would be grossly self-deceiving to deny that your world and mine revolve around anything other than the ordinary sense of "me." As a spiritual practice, I would suggest following your own self-centeredness down, as it were, to its deepest roots. Don't waste your time making judgments about other people—which would be self-serving—or trying to figure them out, as if you can. Just set your mind on being honest about yourself, without creating a fuss. Very likely, you'll find the primitive urge for self-preservation staring you in the face, or some twisted version of it. This is in all probability what Saint Paul was talking about. Yoga philosophy ranks self-preservation with food, sex, and sleep, and it is woven tightly around them too. This instinct is obviously good and necessary, but it often rears its head in unexpected places—especially where issues of control are concerned—that have little or no relation to actual survival.

Let me make a few more basic distinctions that might help you sort this out. Through *self-examination*, we turn our attention to our failings and shortcomings, as well as our positive gifts, so we can understand ourselves better and make changes that need to be made. The purpose of self-examination is *not* to magnify the meaning of what we see, giving it a significance that is out of proportion to the reality of our lives. This would indicate self-absorption too; and anyone who makes a habit of it should consider giving up self-examination as a Lenten fast! Think of *self-awareness* as a process of personal growth in which we become less self-absorbed, less selfish, and less self-centered—even to the point of becoming transparent to ourselves. In the same way, I do not want your Lenten practice to make you self-conscious in the company of others. *Self-consciousness* can be so paralyzing that it qualifies as a form of evil. Why? Because we become frozen by it, and never become who we are meant to be.

Also, keep in mind that the spiritual path is not an advanced course in *self-improvement,* which, when completed, gives us the ability or the wisdom to reach down within ourselves and pull out the roots of our self-centeredness. Our theologies, theories, and therapies can greatly improve the human condition, but we're all quite skilled at hiding behind them too—behind what we believe we know. That's why it's better and more reliable to apply the energy of your life to improving the lives of others in concrete ways, while praying, deeply, about your own life and theirs.

With regard to your Lenten spiritual practice, my suggestion is to follow a structured pattern of self-examination and prayer, and stay with it—perhaps fifteen minutes set aside each morning or evening for self-examination, followed by fifteen minutes of prayer. I hope you will use the Prayer of the Heart that I recommended a few weeks ago:

Lord Jesus Christ, Son of God, have mercy on me, a sinner.

Simply repeat the prayer with loving-kindness and devotion. Once this time of daily self-examination and prayer is completed, then let it go until the next day. The only exception might be when a specific problem area arises; if this happens, then we can discuss it as a separate matter. The important point is simply to do the spiritual practice regularly, which is the difficult part. Our minds always create reasons to avoid or delay the practice. Of course, it's entirely possible that those reasons might be good; your insightful comment on the danger of self-absorption being a case in point. The self-examination you have done so far has revealed the truth of it: you know what it feels like to be thinking about yourself too much, turning your attention within when your help is needed elsewhere. But this is not a good reason to discontinue the prayer.

Make a spiritual discipline of this prayer, and you will soon discover that it's not so much "you" who prays (although this is obviously true), but that the prayer is praying you—or the Spirit is praying through you. This is the beauty of the spiritual path—it puts us in a position where the answers find us. And that is also why I insist that you follow the path, rather than spend too much time reading about it. Reading is good, but if you actually follow the spiritual path, then you will eventually discover that its goal does not revolve around "you" and "me." The path is about the presence of God.

Another benefit of the Prayer of the Heart will be your strengthened capacity to witness your life not only while you're praying, but also throughout the day. I realize this probably seems unrelated to anything obviously "religious." However, on the spiritual path it is extremely helpful to observe our inner thoughts and feelings without making judgments about them. I would suggest that moral judgments are only one part of a devout and faithful life. In practice, we have all kinds of judgmental thoughts that are thoroughly inappropriate and rarely under our control, including those we never give an outward voice. So while you pray, simply witness your thoughts when they arise, without judging them. Observe and learn. Investigate yourself while you pray. Investigate your life, just as you open your heart to the presence of God. Receive the joy and inner peace that will inevitably come; and above all else, do not start thinking, under any circumstances, that God has singled you out for special gifts and revelations. The Prayer of the Heart will help you overcome any unruly judgments you might make about yourself and others, and this will not only clear your mind, but also strengthen your faith.

Someday, you may discover the luminous presence that exists within every person. This presence is a great mystery, and part of the Holy Mystery. Whether this is the "Christ who lives in me" that Saint Paul talked about is a question I cannot answer. It may be. I do know that this awareness within is not the "me" or "you" that we routinely experience. It is unquestionably sacred, but I would advise against calling it the face or form of God. Otherwise, you might claim it for yourself and become entangled in those self-absorbing thoughts you alluded to so perceptively. You may encounter this Mystery, and others like it, if you stay on the spiritual path long enough. Whether they will provide you with any helpful insights about "the self" is a question that only you can answer.

Like I said, I've been hesitant to discuss "the self" in an abstract or philosophical way. It seems to me that we learn about God and whatever "the self" might be through the heart, and the heart of God is love. The pursuit of love in all relationships, from the smallest acts of kindness to the most courageous stands for justice, eventually unveils the luminous presence within us all, as well as our tenacious self-centeredness. I hope you will take this seriously: the love of God draws us closer to the light, but it also makes the darkness of Good Friday much easier to see. So, when you find that light, do your best to live in its presence, because the darkness will not be far behind.

Your question about self-absorption is excellent, and I'm glad you asked it. The most helpful thing I can say is simply to be vigilant on the spiritual path, especially with regard to "the self." Millions of years of human evolution have honed our self-deceiving skills with great precision. Humankind is Holy Mystery: our lives can reveal the glory of God, but we can also be astonishingly treacherous. If I were you, I would do my best to remember that both are true.

Faithfully yours.

Holy Week

13. THE DARK NIGHT

My Dear Friend,

I am so pleased to receive your note. I'm pleased that you're talking about your life again, that you're talking with your family, and that you're breaking out of your hard shell. You call this "courage." I call it "love." We're both talking about the same thing. And I am just as pleased by your intriguing comments concerning Good Friday: Jesus overcomes the darkness, the world, and death itself. You're right. Then comes the next, more intimidating part—we are meant to make the passage too.

I know how troubled you feel about this. To sense darkness within ourselves is supposed to be troubling—disquietude, restlessness, the feeling that something isn't right, fear of the unknown. Many people on the spiritual path experience some version of it. As to why this is happening to you now, I cannot give a definitive answer. Difficult inner struggles, grief, personal tragedies—these might trigger it, but so can deep joy and love. Sometimes the Spirit makes it happen for reasons only the Spirit knows. I do remember an old saying that might be helpful: "The more we try to do good, the closer the darkness seems to be." It seems unfair and contradictory, but it's often true. There's another possibility I would consider.

Maybe the Spirit wants to break open that shell of yours even more! This could happen. Would it be absurd to say that you are on the right path *and* you may be more troubled in the weeks and months ahead? That Good Friday really is "good," even when we are the ones making the passage? Or that there's no reason to be afraid? That is exactly what I'm telling you.

I have to laugh. I've encouraged you to share more of your life with those you love, which you have clearly done. Now, you ask me to do the same, and I'm the one who hesitates. Why? For one, "the darkness" is an uneasy topic of conversation. In fact, I would not suggest discussing this with your family, at least not anytime soon, and not until you consider what you want to say several times. Despite our supposedly "rational" culture, thick layers of fear and superstition surround this subject. On top of that, those troubling feelings can be confused with depression. Honestly, I would not pursue this with you here except for my confidence in your sensitivity and good judgment. I also have another reason. When all this first happened to me, I had no idea that "the dark night of the soul" existed. I knew the biblical passage "It is a terrible thing to fall into the hands of the living God" (Hebrews 10:31, NLT), but never would I have dreamed that something so terrible might land on my doorstep and turn out to be so good. Over a span of four or five months, I vacillated between believing I was dying and going crazy. To be blunt, "dying to the world" sums up pretty well what "the passage" is actually like. Only later did I appreciate that this "cleansing," which is mysterious enough, reaches deeper into a person's soul than our usual ideas about "sin" can explain. Yes, these are the right words: "dark night," "cleansing," and "sin." Nevertheless, the passage is also creative, liberating, and revealing of life's meaning. My point is that anyone in this situation needs assistance, especially from a spiritual friend, and this can be hard to find.

Remember that no one has all the answers—certainly not me. I can share my experience; I can tell you what happened to me and how *my* life was transformed. I can tell you as a matter of faith and experience that the light is not overcome by the darkness. And if you want reassurance from an ordinary person that anyone can make the passage, then I gladly give it. Beyond that, everything becomes speculative and presumptuous. My part in this letter is to be as honest as I can; yours is to pray *and* think for yourself. I'm serious. Too much certainty in these matters can be dangerously misleading. Are you surprised I'm saying this? Would you rather hear me state categorically that darkness is "evil" and light is "good," and leave it at that? It would be definite and clear, but offer little practical help—and it might steer you away from the direction you need to go. Why? Because "the darkness" is not what it appears to be. It represents those parts of ourselves that need to be redeemed, and this means that perceiving the darkness is not just good, it's profoundly good.

It's early Saturday morning, nearly twenty-five years ago. I'm waiting for my hot shower to fill the bathroom with steam. Glancing to my left, I see a bright sun shining through the window. A few moments later, rays of light pierce the moist air, leaving traces of rainbow colors on the wall. I love life. I love everything about it. I step into the shower and enjoy the water falling upon my head and face. This is my last memory before everything changes. My body shudders. Reaching out to the wall for support, I stand there, motionless. Intuitively, I know that something important and spiritual has just happened, but this is quickly forgotten as the weakness in my limbs becomes more apparent. Slowly, I draw back the curtain and look at the sink and mirror against the far wall. My eyesight is fine, although objects in the bathroom—a toothbrush, the glass in the mirror, the bright color of the walls—seem vivid in their details. I think that I'm seeing them for the first time, and then wonder if it might be my last. For a second, I smile at my sometimes bad habit of joking about almost anything. Realizing that I still might fall and injure myself, I turn off the shower and make my way, half-crawling, to the sofa in the next room. I remain there for the rest of the day, trying to understand what is going on.

One day becomes two, three, and then a week. It seems unusual to feel drained physically, yet attentive and alert. This is nothing compared with my deep, persistent, and, at times, teary spiritual longing. Longing of this kind is like an illness—a wound to the soul. I feel isolated, cut off, and strangely disconnected from the life I love so much. Occasionally, it becomes manifest in physical symptoms. Mild burning sensations erupt into body aches and fevers. These episodes disappear as quickly as they arise. My usual enjoyment of food is all but gone. Long, solitary walks help to ease my mind and keep my body working. Apart from this semblance of activity, I have little interest in doing anything. Ordinary conversation is painful. I do my best to fulfill duties and responsibilities, which means showing up when and where I'm expected. Friends comment on my pale and shrunken appearance. This is their polite way of saying I should see a doctor, and when I do, nothing is clinically wrong. My longing grows stronger, and I can't explain the feeling that my life seems to be withering away. I don't really believe that I'm dying, but I know that I could if this torturous sickness continues. My emotions are a mess, and with every passing day I become more concerned, and more afraid. All this describes how I first perceive the darkness within myself, the longing, and a growing fear of the unknown.

Over the next two months, I gradually accept the situation, which means facing a reality I cannot change, without giving in to despair. It's amazing how much we pray when the possibility of death seems close by—and how focused our attention becomes. My waking hours are spent reviewing every part of my life and sorting through every possible sin. Think of "sin" as anything that separates us from God's love, and you can appreciate how far self-examination can go. My secret sins—hurtful, destructive, inconsiderate things I have done—are easy to confess. I think of others who were involved and how they must have felt. Then I simply turn to God and say, "Yes, this happened, and I am truly sorry." I call some people to apologize. As it turns out, the smaller, more ambiguous memories prove to be considerably more tenacious and troublesome. In my youth, an unhappy relative told me that people never really fulfill their dreams. These are spirit-killing words, disguised as the voice of experience and wisdom. I remember thinking, "What a miserable person." I feel sorry for him, while resenting the fact that he would make such a horrible comment. I think about this a long time, finally acknowledging my anger and disappointment with him. Emotional wounds like these are not "sins," but they can have a powerful, undermining influence on our lives. On an even deeper level, I find a difficult nest of emotions involving fear: the fear of being blamed, for example, or wrongly accused, and the feeling that I won't be met with approval by God or anyone else. Occasionally, these raw emotions are released in dreams or spontaneously when

I walk or pray. These several weeks are intense and painful, yet I begin to feel lighter, more settled inside, and free of accumulated guilt and frustration.

By now, I recognize the cleansing that is taking place, and I expect my condition to improve. This is *not* what happens. My previously vague sense of inner darkness suddenly takes on the appearance of a substantial presence. While I'm walking, in the middle of the day, an utter pitch-blackness fills my field of vision. My first reaction is pure terror. It's not so much the color that's so awful, but the feeling of emptiness and void. I can't adequately describe this, except to say that the darkness is a world in itself. When it draws close, my "self"—the person I know myself to be—seems to shatter. I run to relieve my anxiety. Actually, I'm trying to run away. While I'm running, the thought crosses my mind that I'm being pursued, which sounds absolutely crazy. I know it's crazy, and then I realize that I'm running from the unknown within myself. For the next month or more, I'm exasperated, emotionally spent, and physically worn out. My longing for God persists, but I have little concern, if any, with personal sins and no real desire to pray. Sometimes my body aches. Pressure rises from the pit of my stomach, up into my neck and head. It's terrible when this happens, but suddenly, it disappears for reasons I can't understand. Finally, I find something that really helps. I go outside, find an isolated place where I'm undisturbed by others, and stretch out on the earth. I just lie there, flat on my back, and give myself to God, without thinking anything. I can't emphasize enough how restorative this is. Eventually, I recognize it as a form of prayer—more in-my-body than before, but deeper and, quite literally, grounding.

The more I pray this way, the more attuned I become to the

silence within me—in the space between my thoughts. By now, I'm tired of thinking anything, which makes the silence both a welcome refuge and an unexpected source of relaxation and happiness. When my attention turns to my thoughts, I understand them from a different point of view. I'm not thinking *about* my thoughts or *about* myself. Instead, I'm witnessing my thoughts as they actually arise. This is a significant breakthrough in itself—a breakthrough in understanding, rather than an emotional release. I realize that these ordinary thoughts are the gift we have been given to use, for better or worse. "The world" is out there all right, but that's not the most revealing part. By the power of our thinking, in the broadest sense, we create "worlds" that include images and ideas about who we are. They penetrate our minds, bodies, and souls, define reality, and offer enough makeshift security to impair our spiritual vision, leaving us nearly blind or asleep, spiritually, and relatively content with the way things are. Our thoughts "think" us. But these "worlds" we create are not the totality of who we are. They're not the gift we have been given, but evidence of the gift; and they're definitely not God.

A week or so later, when I'm walking along the sidewalk, the darkness appears a second time. It swells up within me as pressure felt within my body. I no longer care what the darkness is; whether it's an unconscious projection of the mind or a supernatural entity makes no difference whatsoever. I sense sweaty fear in my flesh; but my awareness of it seems separate and detached. Without reflecting, I willfully submit to the reality of the situation, without surrendering in any way. Instead of running, I simply stop to face whatever "it" is, and in that moment several things happen: the darkness disappears with my fear, and the shattered pieces of my life begin to make sense. I understand that the incident in the shower, months before, is the Spirit breaking me open, accomplishing something that none of us can do on our own. I understand that we do not "survive" the passage, at least in the sense of becoming happier versions of the same people we had once been. The passage is not about survival— not maintaining who we are and the way things are—but transformation, and the outcome depends on God and how we respond. Some part of us dies; another part lives on.

I dream of a young boy walking up a steep mountain path. The land is barren. The sky is pitch-black. Approaching the summit, he turns and motions to me with his hand. He wants me to follow. Then he points toward the entrance of a cave at the end of the path. A fiery red glow is all that can be seen within the cave. As I peer into the opening, I realize two things: this is where I have been during the last few months, and this is also where I'm going. He turns, smiles, and the dream ends. After a few days, when I'm standing over the sink, washing dishes, my body shudders again, just as in the shower, and my vision is suddenly filled with the same red color of the cave. Now, an older man sits quietly within the redness, praying. His look invites me to join him. I put down the dishes, and go into the next room, where I sit quietly, praying and reflecting for the rest of the day. The very next morning, just before getting out of bed, I'm thinking of the last four or five months and the dreams. It's a peaceful time of day. The morning is quiet. This is when the sense of approaching darkness occurs a third and final time.

Somehow I know that all these months of struggle, fear, and prayer have merged into a single moment—and that moment has arrived. I gird myself by asking God to be present with me. It happens very quickly. The darkness comes so close that it seems to touch my soul. I remember crying out instinctively, praying that I might be found filled with love—only love. The possibility of death is accepted as the fact of life it has always been; my thoughts come to an end; and the world falls away. The darkness is very different now. It envelops me like a soothing, protective blanket—God is in the darkness too. For a few seconds, maybe more, I lose consciousness. When I awaken, a single thread of light moves within the darkness, dancing at the root of a tree unlike all others. This is not seen with the eyes, not literally, yet it is seen. The light rises above the tree, forming into a luminous face that whispers the secret buried so long ago in our hearts, "I love you. Do not be afraid." In this way, the Spirit teaches us how to pray and how to live; and in hearing, we are free to forgive and we are forgiven—for our sins, for the years of hiding. I walk down the hallway, slowly, to the sofa. Resting there, the room is filled with radiant clear light, laced with gold. Everything else has now fallen away—everything except love.

Like I said before, if you want reassurance that anyone can make the passage, then I gladly give it. It really is that terrible. It really is that good. I can also tell you this: Jesus reveals every bit of it, stretched on the cross, when he says so simply, "Father, forgive them." In that moment, the world is overcome.

Faithfully yours.

The Season of Easter

14. The Leap into Joy

My Dear Friend,

I hope you've enjoyed some time away with your family. A change of scenery now and again can be surprisingly good for the soul. The roses always smell so good upon our return, and we realize how little we noticed them before. Welcome home!

For several days, I've been thinking about a conversation I once had with a close friend. She is a beautiful human being, who reminds me of you in many ways. When we spoke, it was a sunny Easter day, like the one we just had. I was standing on the front steps of the church. She walked up, we greeted each other, probably exchanged a few words about the nice weather, and then she told me something profoundly moving: "My faith has been my strength for many years. It's carried me through some terrible times. But the joy of Easter, the joy of the resurrection—I really don't know about that. It seems out of reach."

That's how our conversation began. Her words caught me completely by surprise. She was the last person on earth I would have expected to say those words. The faith of this woman was as great as that of anyone I've ever known. In her younger days, there were times when she lived on faith alone because she had no food. As an adult, when life was better, this same faith grew into a healthy, even inspiring way of life. It gave her a good nature, a sound mind, and a wonderful sense of humor. I considered these to be true spiritual gifts in her, and others saw her in the same light. They sought out her infectious smile and listening ear because her spirit raised theirs. Her joy made them joyful. For all those reasons, her sincere and honest comment left me dumbfounded.

Soon, I realized that this would be an extraordinary conversation. As it often happens when struggles of the soul come to the surface, she drew a broad picture of her life in my mind by revealing several things at once. She described the world in which she, her family, and the great majority of people live—a world of horrible uncertainty about money for food and medical expenses. She let me know that the kind of deep spiritual joy proclaimed on Easter day, which she wanted, seemed to be a remote possibility for her and most people she knew. Comfort and salvation—yes. But spiritual joy? The more we talked, the more I sensed that she was probing the boundaries of her experience and mine, watching closely to see how I would react to the questions she really wanted to ask: "Is it okay to be happy? Is it selfish to want spiritual joy for ourselves, and to seek it, while so many people suffer?" That is what she wanted to know, and it was no passing concern. *She really wanted to know.*

It took considerable courage for my friend to say all this, and she showed uncommon respect for the sacred nature of the subject she raised. Even so, our conversation barely touched the depth of her questions. It had to be that way. We both knew how complicated life and the human heart can be. We both knew that people who seem to be happy all the time often hide behind a mask. Still, this conversation took an unexpected turn. She had the foresight and wisdom to clear the air of any misconceptions I might have. We were talking about deep spiritual joy, and her words pointed, quite clearly, to one of the most difficult passages on the spiritual path. Actually, it may be the most difficult passage of all. Is it selfish to want this joy? Is it a fantasy to think I could have it? The fact that she was discussing it so openly told me how far she had come and how close she was to finding her answer. Anyone who can feel the depth of her struggle within themselves will be transported to the very same place. In that moment, she was looking within herself and peering into the empty tomb of Jesus. She had seen it; she knew what it meant; and, like all of us—she hesitated in fear and disbelief.

The answer to my friend's question is "definitely yes." It is okay to be happy, and it's okay to want deep spiritual joy for ourselves— the joy beyond joy. It's okay to seek it, and it's okay to receive it. That's the first thing I said to my friend. All spiritual traditions say this: Do not postpone your awakening! Receive the Holy Spirit! Enter the Kingdom of God. When the opportunity comes, do not hesitate or delay. From a spiritual point of view, this is so self-evident that further discussion about it seems silly and absurd. Yet there is no quick and easy route from our everyday lives to the fulfillment of our hope and faith.

Her questions call out the story of Mary, the mother of Jesus, and Mary Magdalene after the crucifixion. The gospels give differing accounts of what they did and saw in the empty tomb, but it is clear that when the other disciples remained in hiding, these two women took the risk of faith. They ventured out into the unknown, which required tremendous courage, and they discovered that the way things seem to be is not always the same thing as the way things are. What they found was an empty tomb, and according to some accounts, an angel. Did they jump for joy? No. They were confused and afraid, just like my friend.

Have you ever wondered about this fear, the hesitation, the impulse to run away when the presence of God is near? Peter, James, and John were afraid when they saw Jesus, radiant with light, on the Mount of the Transfiguration. The disciples knew the prophecies; they had seen his miracles many times; some had seen Lazarus raised from the dead. You might think, after all this, they would not have been so afraid or surprised by the empty tomb. We can come up with any number of explanations, all of them quite rational. Perhaps they were afraid that his body had been stolen. Maybe they were afraid of being arrested. This is all well and good. The possibility of the miraculous defied rational explanation long before the Age of Reason, just as our speculations about their fear don't really explain anything. They only explain it away.

I told my friend that the empty tomb is not an easy place to reach. If it was easy, then the spiritual path would not be needed. When we do reach it, our minds tell us, at first, that we're not supposed to be there. Very likely, we'll run away and hide. To stand before the empty tomb is to meet the promise of deep spiritual joy face to face. I don't mean to be facetious, but therapy might actually be helpful when we find ourselves before our own empty tombs. It could help us sort out our inner confusion and face our fears; but, of course, this depends just as much on the life experience of the therapist or the priest as it does on us. Either way, I wanted her to understand that the empty tomb is not a personal problem to be solved, but a leap of faith to be made—and this leap of faith is a leap into joy.

A great deal of spiritual writing points directly to this leap into joy. Some of it can be as confusing as the passage itself. Stories told about Saint Francis come to mind, but there are many others. Saint Francis strongly encouraged his friends to be joyful at all times—as a sign of faith. Taken at face value, this kind of "encouragement" seems utterly unrealistic, and perhaps a little crazy, obnoxious, and patronizing. As much as we would like to be perpetually joyful, we both know that we aren't. Speaking for myself, I don't consider this to be a personal failing; and quite honestly, I don't believe that Francis was joyful every minute of the day. Historical records clearly tell us that the latter part of his life was filled with emotional anguish and physical pain—not to mention his struggle with the stigmata!

So was Saint Francis being hypocritical when he encouraged us to be joyful every moment? I think not, and I don't believe he was being moralistic or judgmental about how we "should" be feeling. There was a sound method within the appearance of his madness. People who follow the spiritual path can be exceedingly practical people—practical in the way the Spirit perceives life's meaning. They guide us through the delicate web of illusions and delusions that make up so much of our lives. They know our emotions can be a genuine source of divine inspiration and guidance, when acted upon properly. They also know how powerful our emotions can be— powerful enough to define the whole nature of reality for us. Generally, we're stuck in our emotions, especially in our worries and fears, or we find ourselves confused about what our feelings actually are, while struggling with what we believe they should be.

None of this suggests that we're doing anything wrong— nothing whatsoever. In fact, my friend's question, "Is it okay to want this joy, and to seek it, when so many people suffer?" indicates an incisive, caring, and balanced mind at work, which is essential for anyone on the spiritual path. She was a devout Christian, and she simply wanted to experience deep spiritual joy. Yet she was afraid of the possibly selfish motives that might be lurking behind her desire. These are good spiritual instincts. These same instincts carried her through tremendous hardships in life, through every obstacle on the spiritual path, and to the empty tomb of Easter. The question now is how would she respond? How will we respond? Will we make the leap?

Put yourself in her shoes. You're peering into the empty tomb, which is the pivotal moment on the spiritual path. It's already an accomplishment to come this far. It's a sign of God's grace and helping hand in every part of our lives. What are we going to do now? Turn away because of fear? Lose hope or give up because the tomb is empty? We might, but this is precisely when Saint Francis encourages us to be joyful. He knows that we're always standing before our empty tomb. Our first impulse is to project our illusory fears and desires into the emptiness, creating all over again a world that revolves around "me" and "you." This is the world Jesus overcame on the cross. The leap into joy is made here. It can only be here, into the emptiness. The tomb is good because it is empty, and the last thing we want to do is fill it with illusions about ourselves. But that's exactly what we do. We fill our empty tombs with "my" desire, "my" faith, "my" fears, "my" religion. The purpose of the spiritual path is to free us from this lesser world of our own making, and help us make the leap into joy.

Even the most faithful person can have difficulty accepting this impossible possibility: *that God is more than human emotion, that God is more than our idea of God.* Although most everyone would completely agree with that, at least in principle, the way we actually live suggests the exact opposite. We believe one thing, while doing something else.

This is why spiritual traditions warn against seeking religious "experiences," and the reason Saint Francis encourages us to be joyful all the time. He's talking about God, not experiences of God. He's talking about the desire to be free from desire. To seek anything else is to make "how I feel" the object of our attention and devotion. This is the equivalent of filling the empty tomb with images of ourselves, instead of searching for the resurrected Jesus. The end result is that we worship our emotions—in effect, ourselves. It's enticing and seductive, but only because the emotions are so powerful. To follow the spiritual path is to take responsibility for this fact of human life. We do this as an act of moral responsibility and faith, but much more than that is involved: the empty tomb is the place where our spiritual freedom is won.

My friend's question was exactly right: Is it okay to want spiritual joy, and to seek it, while there is so much suffering? The answer is definitely yes. As contradictory as this sounds, we must not only want it, but we must want it passionately. We must want freedom from desire so much that we're willing to give up a world that revolves around "me"; and our self-centeredness goes much deeper than we might think. We must want it enough to give our whole being to God. We will never find this joy as long as we want it for ourselves, or by seeking it to escape from the world's suffering. If we avoid suffering, then we lose the capacity to feel. And if we lose that, we also lose the possibility of deep spiritual joy.

Think of Jesus' crucifixion, and add to his the thousands more crucifixions and killings that took place in those horrific years, and today. Outrage is the right response, not joy. To glorify his suffering for the sake of God makes all the killings, then and now, easier to overlook. You have to wonder whether glorifying the cross really is the spiritual path, or an empty tomb filled with my feelings, my religion, and my faith—all my excuses for not making the leap into joy.

It may take a lifetime. The two Marys were very close to Jesus, and even they didn't make it right then and there. Concerning my friend's question—are we selfish in trying, even when we fail? I don't think so. Each in our own way, we learn to claim our empty tombs for what they truly are; and then, when we're ready, we all can make the leap into joy. We may be afraid to try—afraid that we're doing something wrong, perhaps convincing ourselves that it's all a fantasy. We are afraid. But I want to have the courage of the two Marys, and my friend on the steps of the church. They were afraid, but their lives were not ruled by fear. I do not want to seek joy because I'm afraid of tragedy and suffering. Fear is part of our lives, which makes it part of the spiritual path—and the love of God casts out fear. I think Jesus is telling us to make the leap.

Faithfully yours.

15. HOPE

My Dear Friend,

I hope you realize that not every church you run across focuses on "the end of the world," as you put it. I'm aware of grim news in the world and of predictions about the end of it all, but I like to remember Jesus' teaching on prophecies: "You know how to interpret the appearance of earth and sky, but why do you not know how to interpret the present time?" (Luke 12:56, NSRV). Of course biblical quotations may have their cryptic side, and this may be one of them. So what do you think "the present time" means? Maybe Jesus was speaking of his own present time, rather than ours, but he's not here to ask. Or I could give some down-to-earth advice by encouraging you to focus on the pressing issues of our day. This only raises another question: What exactly does our "present time" involve? And if I concede that our present time is in terrible shape, which I'm certainly willing to do, then what have I actually said? Not very much. Surely anyone with an open heart and mind, whether an ordinary person or a prophet, can see the obvious. Let's say that the future turns out much worse than we imagine now—or better. Either way, when that time comes, God will still be God, and we'll still be wondering what tomorrow will bring.

I share your worry about the way the world is going and your passion for doing something about it. I only hope you can resist letting despair undermine your faith today. The future is definitely at stake—we can be sure of that—but so is the present. I am a hopeful person. The spiritual path is hopeful, yet this hope involves more than finding reasons to hope in a future that *might* be, more than dissatisfaction with the way things are, and more than opinions fired back and forth by the spiritual soothsayers. We both know *for a fact* that the future will reveal the consequences of our actions now, for better or worse.

Have you considered the possibility that the world might be renewing itself in "this present time"—calling out compassion and loving-kindness, rather than "spirituality" wrapped in fear and despair? This is what I want you to remember: the day that comes tomorrow will be another today. And if the spiritual path is not followed today, then it is never followed. It's the present time, the eternal present—always the present—that needs our love and compassion. How else can the world change for the better, unless we open our hearts to perceive the presence of God in the here and now?

There's another saying attributed to Jesus that I like very much. It's a little cryptic too, but it calls our attention to the eternal presence of God in all things:

> *I am the light shining upon all things. I am the sum of everything, for everything has come forth from me, and towards me everything unfolds. Split a piece of wood, and there I am. Pick up a stone and you will find me there.* (THE GOSPEL OF THOMAS, LOGION 77)

Reflect on this, prayerfully. Even one glimpse of God's eternal presence, by just one person, or two or three, can make the difference between a world ending and a world beginning again. It all depends on what you see in the world, and what you think it means.

The last place we would expect to find signs of hope is the New York City subway. For people who live elsewhere, like yourself, the subway conjures images of subterranean crime and filth or a place one visits at the risk of death. Fortunately, I was given the opportunity to live in Manhattan for nearly fifteen years, and I'm the better for it. The subway I love is a microcosm of life aboveground, seen below, but more raw and intimate. Everyone comes into close contact with everyone else: the homeless rub shoulders with Wall Street bankers; government leaders, with store clerks and cooks; and all with diverse complexions, political views, nationalities, and religions. A person who shows disrespect for someone else on the subway may meet with disapproval or be corrected by a fellow passenger. First-time visitors may find this rude or shocking, but the well-known stereotype is true: New Yorkers will often tell you what they think. This distinctive combination of intimacy and honesty makes life in Manhattan open-minded and unexpectedly humane. This is "normal" life in the City. So, regardless of your less than positive impression of Manhattan—that it would be the last place on earth to find "signs" of real hope—let me tell you this: I was not alone in witnessing what I am about to tell you.

I was taking the No. 1 train in the afternoon, traveling between the Cathedral of St. John the Divine on 110th Street, where I worked, to my apartment on 66th. One hand firmly held the upright silver pole inside the train; the other was holding my newspaper. At the 96th Street stop, I watched three families enter the train. Each family consisted of a parent pushing a small child in a stroller—three parents (two mothers, one father), three children, three strollers. It became apparent, rather quickly, that they were strangers who had coincidentally stepped into the same subway car at the same time. As the door closed behind them, the parents positioned their strollers into a small circle. At first, this created an image of "circling the wagons," but, in fact, it was the most practical solution to the limited space available to them. The children were facing each other in a tightly formed circle. The parents stood behind their strollers, holding each one securely in their hands. The children sat comfortably and quietly, while their parents stood there watchfully.

The stage was set. Several other passengers joined me in noticing the small circle of children with their parents. It was the silence, I think, that drew our attention first, yet there was a feel in the air— the expectation that something *will happen* whenever people gather in a circle. We all watched, without really staring, and waited to see what this expected something was going to be. Our intuition was right. One child had a small box of popcorn in his lap. Slowly, he grasped the box, and then, reaching out with his hand, he offered some of his popcorn to the child on his right, who reached in, took a piece or two, and ate it.

Not a sound was made. A few seconds passed, and the third child, who had some pink candy in her lap, offered some to the child who had the popcorn. He took a few bits of the pink candy in his hand and began to eat. Again, not a sound was made. From their point of view, this was no big deal. The parents watched it happen, along with most everyone else. Smiles were forming all around.

The children did this entirely on their own, without asking permission or making a fuss. Perhaps we shouldn't be surprised, yet in the moment, it seemed as if a miracle was happening before our eyes.

The children continued, sharing their food among themselves, eating contentedly—just living in a way that came naturally to them. About that time, the three parents began to feel uneasy with the situation. They were concerned about issues of health and hygiene, and probably feeling anxious about strangers. In a movement that seemed to have been choreographed, all of the parents motioned to their children to stop sharing their food. As onlookers, we could sense that the parents felt reluctant about this, but it seemed to be the responsible thing to do. Perhaps a minute passed. Not a sound was made by the children, and then they began to share their food once again. There was nothing defiant or showy about it. They were just sharing their food and being hospitable. Two of the parents noticed it, which made them giggly; but once again, they all motioned for their children to stop.

Remarkably, the whole sequence was repeated yet again. All three kids were sharing popcorn and pink candy. This time, the parents laughed out loud. The children carried on just as before, smiling a little with their parents, and having their feast of kid food on the 1 train. By now, most everyone in our part of the subway was smiling. Some were openly laughing. We had witnessed an incredible event, and we knew it. Everyone would have agreed with the parents' reasonable fears about hygiene and strangers. Still, the question of whether the children should be stopped from sharing their food stared back at us all. If the right decision was to stop them, then we, as a people, are in a great deal of trouble, morally and spiritually, and a lot of hungry people will have a future even more bleak than it is now. As the event unfolded, the moral questions became less an issue of reason and rationality, and more a sign of the Spirit's presence. The Spirit overcame any reason to stop them, and it broke through all the other ideas we—the grown-ups—had about the world.

The train arrived at the next stop. The door opened. One parent moved her child and stroller onto the platform; another moved a few steps down the aisle. The sacred circle dissolved as quickly as it had formed, but the traces of that small miracle were forever etched in our memory. All those children did was to share their food with some strangers, and this released pure joy in everyone who witnessed it. This joy was wrapped in hope and offered as a gift from the Spirit. No one who received this gift—not the children, not the parents, not the onlookers—was willing to give it back.

If, in this "present time," we feel despair at what we see, then remember that it is the Spirit—God's Spirit—who sustains and renews everything that exists. The Spirit is real, not in the way that "facts" are used to support prophecy or science, but as the Spirit within us knows the "real" to be. When we look with open hearts, we begin to see it; and in our seeing, we are changed. We know what to do in times like ours. Like those marvelous children, we can do it. They are true signs of hope in this present time. Even in the underground world of the New York subway, fear and hopelessness fall away under the irresistible power of joy. We can find it everywhere we look. Split open a log. Pick up a rock. Take a ride on the subway.

Faithfully yours.

·❧ III ❧·

THE PATH OF LOVE

The Season of Pentecost

16. A Spiritual Home

My Dear Friend,

For months, Asha and I have eagerly anticipated the arrival of spring. And then it came—with a fury. One heavy overnight rain melted nearly all the snow in the surrounding hills, which resulted in a severe flood. Since then, we've had very little rain, and the rivers are running very low. Yet my lawn, with no fertilizer, somehow defies the dry ground with luxuriant, bright green growth. This, of course, means less fishing and more mowing. The better news is that a familiar pair of phoebes have, once again, made their home above the windowsill on my porch. They either renovate their magnificent moss-covered nest from the previous year, or build a new one only a few feet away. Their return each year is more pleasing than I can say. Each day, regardless of my worries or pressing concerns, I can look at my windowsill and see an intricate web of pattern and purpose woven through their lives and mine. The Spirit's presence can be seen everywhere—in the change of the seasons, the unpredictable rain, the homebound phoebes, and, my friend, in you and me. The Spirit is present in us all, drawing us closer to the place we are meant to be.

I think of you when I see the phoebes. You've been looking for a "spiritual home"—that is, a church where you can pray, reflect, and meet people. Based on what I read in your letter, you haven't been very successful. Keep looking. You'll find the right place. We live in difficult times, though, and people can be on edge, even at church— especially there. I'll make some suggestions about what to look for, but my main concern is with how you conduct yourself while you're looking. I'll tell you why: I don't want you to become disenchanted. Disenchantment has a tendency to linger, and then fester, until it transforms into cynicism about life itself. I've known people who have given up religion and eventually left the spiritual path for this reason alone. I want you to understand that the spiritual path and the spiritual home are not the same, and they should not be confused— although they easily are. The nature of the spiritual path you actually follow—which is what I mean by "how you conduct yourself"—will take you to the home you're meant to find. So just keep your eye on the path, and remember that there's no substitute for the faith a person lives by every day, wherever your "home" may be.

Here are my suggestions. First, it seems to me that your struggle with "the God question" over these last few months has revealed something of great importance about you. I'm thinking of the significance you give to generosity, hospitality, and an open mind. Apparently the Spirit has been calling you to live by these qualities. The time may also come when you will have to do more than recognize them within yourself. You may be called to defend them. Maybe that time has already come. It has been said that all religion "begins in mysticism and ends in politics," which may be true. The crucifixion was certainly an act of politics in its most debased form; and yet it did not put an end to the life of Christ or mysticism. His resurrection was a beginning, just as your life has begun in a new way. The crucifixion revealed the leading role that ethics and religion must play to create a free, decent, and moral society, and it exposed the folly of reducing the spiritual path to lines drawn between "us" and "them" or believing it can be followed by waving a flag. Give yourself time to think about this, without indulging in disenchantment about religion and politics. Disenchantment can do more than cause people to leave the spiritual path. It can become a religion unto itself—a reason to keep things just the way they are and to feel justified in doing so.

Second, I hope you understand generosity, hospitality, and open-mindedness as more than personal qualities. My advice is to make them your daily spiritual practice. Whenever you feel disenchanted or lost, you can depend on them to keep you on secure footing. In a very practical way, these qualities will help you resist thinking in terms of "us" and "them." I realize that people often think of their spiritual home in exactly this way, but I would strongly advise against it. In fact, the best way to counteract this tendency within yourself is to avoid ordinary gossip. It has a great deal in common with "us versus them" thinking. Gossip is so commonplace that, in the best of circumstances, we tend to dismiss it as insignificant and petty, when, in fact, it is a spiritual disaster. We may tell ourselves that unkind words spoken about someone else will ease our own anxious insecurities. It seems *relatively harmless*. But then, a few unkind words become crass manipulation at the expense of others to make ourselves feel better. It gets worse: if people are talking about someone else, then they aren't talking about me! Or we actually want people to talk about "me" or "us," so we can be the center of their world. We like being seen as "people in the know," which gives the appearance of power and influence. All this "explains" our bad behavior in quasi-rational terms; and yet, the hard fact remains that gossip rehearses a crucifixion, with ourselves in the role of accuser. None of us would ever believe ourselves capable of such destructive behavior in "real life," yet we willingly participate, telling ourselves that our "behind the scenes" and "off the record" comments have been made for the common good. This, of course, is a lie. People are hurt; we know it; and we participate anyway.

I do realize that gossip sometimes serves more positive ends. It can give important information about people that we might need to know—in order to help them. It can help us sort through our own messy feelings about difficult, complicated matters. But do you see the similarity between ordinary gossip and your experience of political manipulation in church? Some high-profile gossip is conducted in full public view, which creates an aura of authority and legitimate "news." It can be heard from the pulpit and on talk radio and television. We may willingly consent to this, despite the fact that our personal involvement, which is usually confined to listening to "experts," seems passive and harmless. Some believe this "news" serves the public interest, sharpens moral clarity, and enhances political debate. What I hear is still plain, ordinary gossip perpetuated by people who claim to be "in the know." Its purpose is to ensure that everyone knows his place and stays there, so everything remains the same. Whether gossip happens only behind the scenes or reaches millions of ears in the name of God and country, it is still a disaster in the making, driven by cynicism and resentment.

This brings me to the crux of my letter, which is your desire to "find just the right place" or to "get it right." Of course you want to be a better person and to follow the spiritual path faithfully. I want this for you too. But be careful when you hear ministers quoting religious texts that encourage us to be "perfect." Quite honestly, the only sense in which I have known perfection in myself or anyone else is "perfectionism"—and this is the one reliable way to make everyone completely miserable, including yourself. Let's just stay with "getting it right," and consider *that* to be perfection in loving-kindness, generosity, and an open mind. That is enough of a challenge. You must decide for yourself what this means for you, but I find it difficult to imagine you as a person who is always "in the know" or on the right side of every issue that comes along.

If you're the kind of person who sets goals on the spiritual path—and I believe you are—then let me emphasize that "getting it right" is one of the most ambiguous and slippery goals you could possibly choose. You have responded to a call in your life, and now you're looking for a spiritual home to support your path. This is a worthy goal in itself, and a big step to take. I want you to realize that a genuine spiritual home will always help you with forgiveness. If you can get it right in forgiveness, then you have followed the path exceedingly well. Jesus put it this way to his disciples: "Receive the Holy Spirit. If you forgive the sins of any, they are forgiven them; if you retain the sins of any, they are retained" (John 20:22–23, NRSV). This should be good news, because we have a lot of forgiving to do, apologies to offer, and amends to make. Try to find a spiritual home that encourages you to receive the Holy Spirit many times and in many ways. You'll need this to get it right in forgiveness. I'm thinking of a place where everything is not cast in stone, where there is more than one way to follow the spiritual path, and where you can live and grow and change your mind. I'm also thinking of a place where you can be born again—not just once, but again and again.

I can hear you asking now: If our first rebirth was real, then why would a second be needed? Isn't one rebirth, one Easter, one Pente-cost enough? Apparently, it's not. Each rebirth is entirely real, but the next can happen much more deeply, even to the point of seriously changing many of our previous beliefs. It can happen exactly that way. Our shadowy side remains throughout, or returns with a vengeance—until, perhaps with enough forgiveness, we finally let go of the presumption that we can "get it right." No one is right about everything or totally right about anything.

The best thing you can do is to listen to your heart. The Spirit will take you where your soul wants to go. In the meantime, I would suggest finding some soulful friends who respect your hospitality, generosity, and open mind in matters of faith, and encourage you to see beyond religious or political loyalties. When you find them, and you will, the home you seek will be very close. You will learn to carry those spiritual friends in your heart; and they will carry you in theirs. And what about the saints and bodhisattvas who have left their bodies in this life: Are they your friends too, your companions on the way? Have they found their home? I believe they have. Yet they return, again and again, like those glorious phoebes, and their lives help us learn to love and to forgive. It's in their nature. It's who they are.

Faithfully yours.

17. WORRY

My Dear Friend,

I am truly pleased that you called. Our conversation affirmed, once again, the blessing that friendship is meant to be, and I am grateful for both—the conversation and the friendship. I'm also pleased by the level of trust that has developed between us. You express your ideas and feelings quite openly, *and* you're willing to reflect on them without being defensive. This was especially evident when our thoughts turned to some troublesome issues: terrorism, the war, the environmental crisis, and paying the bills. Unfortunately, the list is all too familiar and much too long, but life is like that these days. You may remember the distinct tone of worry in your voice and mine as we spoke, which we acknowledged, but never really examined. By then, we had covered a lot of ground, and we both needed to say goodbye. Nevertheless, it is worry itself, rather than the issues we worry about, that's the more difficult obstacle on the spiritual path. If you wish, we can take this up again during another phone call; in the meantime, I want you to know what I would've said, had we had more time.

I should begin by stating the obvious: everyone worries. When people ask me whether they're worrying too much, I always smile and say, "Probably so." I never know exactly what they mean. How could I know? They may have good reasons to worry. All I really know is that a little worry goes a long way, and worrying about worrying does nothing to make the situation any better. As a rule, I don't believe worry is a moral failing, although it usually suggests a lack of trust. This should be obvious too. You don't need to be an expert to know where a large part of our worries come from: an age built on the creed "greed is good," which sets a worrisome tone for everyone, can hardly be called trustworthy. It's the sea the powers-that-be would like us to swim in. The assumption is that you can trust people to be untrustworthy, and that's supposed to be okay. Their greed is thought to be good for everyone. This is nonsense in the disguise of common sense, but it's effective: we all become a little more greedy, a lot more worried, and starved for trust. Worry spins out of control, once you lose your trust in life. As a priest, I worry about that.

Most of my worries lie close to home. Asha and I, for example, live near a state highway that many drivers use as a speedway. My worry is that someone will smash his car into hers when she's on the road. I know Asha is a careful driver. I remind myself of that again and again. I try not to worry, but I still do. On the other hand, when I'm behind the wheel, I worry about the stove. Did I turn off the gas before leaving the house? I can't tell you how many times I've turned the car around and returned just to be sure. Once, I was mortified to find that I had left it on—and once was enough to prove that my worry was justified. Also, I like it when people worry about me, particularly when I'm working too hard or failing to take time off like I should. Their worry means that they care, and that helps me to take better care of myself. Like I said, a little worry goes a long way. At the other extreme, I don't like to be worried over. It feels like control, rather than concern, and I'm pretty good at keeping a healthy distance from controlling people.

The way I see it, those kinds of worries are relatively ordinary, normal, and within reasonable limits, even healthy. Habitual worry, on the other hand, is a very different matter. Some highly educated, well-meaning people have argued that worry becomes an "issue"—that is to say, a habit—among those who have the least to worry about. They're talking about the middle class (whoever that is), economically developed countries, and specifically, Americans. According to this view, if people have a reasonably good life, while millions of others have nothing, then their "normal" worries, by comparison, seem ridiculous and absurd. There's definitely some truth in this point of view, but it distorts as much as it reveals. People I know, both rich and poor, tend to worry about illnesses in their families, paying the bills, their children falling prey to drug dealers, *and* the suffering of people they've never met, in places they've never seen. All these worries seem entirely legitimate to me; and to my knowledge, those same people do the best they can with what they have. The fact that they have advantages that a large part of the world wants—and should have   is a flimsy reason to call their integrity into question, especially when the life they've worked so hard to have seems to be slipping away. I will grant you this: most people, in all walks of life, worry way too much. But it's a great deal more worrisome to hold the wrong people accountable for it—and for all the wrong reasons.

If I were smart, I would leave it at that. I've said just enough to get in trouble, but not enough to address the genuine dilemma that lies behind worry: by keeping our attention fixed on what might happen, or more likely, what we might lose, we fail to appreciate what we actually have. We risk losing the very things we care about the most. This dilemma goes far deeper into the soul than anything materialism and greed can account for. It involves one of our most basic questions about trust: Are we willing to have trust in life or do we reject it? This is no small matter, and the line between them is drawn at the edge of an abyss. Everyone peers into it on occasion, and the still, small voice of wisdom pulls us back. That is why the tone of worry that I heard in both of our voices gets my attention. If you cross that line, you concede your vital energy not just to one particular worry or another, but to the specter of every worry rolled into one, which you very definitely want to avoid. You would lose a very wholesome part of yourself—your trust in life—and then you would be well on your way to becoming a miserable, untrustworthy person. So, either do something about your worries or let them go. Otherwise, they feed on your soul, and they have an insatiable appetite.

Like many people, I became aware of the relation between worry and trust as a young teenager. My family gathered for dinner every day at 5:00 P.M. Exceptions were sometimes made, but the reasons had to be good. The dinner table was a sacred place. There, we worked on, struggled with, and lived out some of the most important skills in living: how to speak freely *and* respectfully, how to listen *and* be heard, how to be aware of yourself *and* others, and how to be yourself *and* help others to be themselves. We talked about everything (almost) around the dinner table: my sister, Wendy, and I sometimes stumbling over our words, eating too fast, and wondering what Mom and Dad were thinking. I especially remember my early teenage years, when the surge of adolescent hormones made my head swim. It was a terrible time for me. Despite my best efforts to be careful, I knocked over my glass of iced tea or milk onto the dinner table so often that it became a family joke. It was embarrassing, but gradually I learned to join in the laughter. As you might guess, once I learned to laugh at myself, the accidents became much less frequent.

The expectation—the unspoken rule written into our hearts—was that any topic of conversation could be brought to the dinner table, as long as we expressed ourselves in a respectful way. There were plenty of disturbances in our lives—family crises, worries, frustrations, fears, and so on—which we did our best to discuss openly. They were meant to be seen, understood, and, when necessary, acted upon. This had to be learned. Learning depended on trust, and trust nurtured some essentially happy, restful minds. The real possibility of inner peace, expressed outwardly at the dinner table, was the heart of our home. We struggled with it, to be sure, and there were unhappy moments. Yet in a true spiritual way, a sense of tranquility *was* home; and for me, it became a doorway to an awareness of God's presence.

Naturally, the wisdom about life that we learn at home becomes "real" when our lives are tested in the world. My test happened about the same time that I was making a mess at the dinner table. My mom and dad gave me their permission to walk anywhere I wanted to go, as long as I was back by dinnertime. At first, I walked to the YMCA on weekdays to play basketball in the gym. One thing led to another, and I discovered that by following the railroad tracks, I could walk from the small town where we lived to a neighboring town about five miles away. It was a great adventure that I made many times, sometimes with friends, and other times, by myself. Along the way, I would put my hands on the tracks, so I could feel the vibration of an approaching train. I loved to do that. A great thrill in my life was to detect the train, and then watch it roar by a few minutes later. For lunch, I took a bottle of Orange Crush and a peanut butter and banana sandwich that I ate by a small pond near the tracks. I loved sitting by the pond too. And after eating, I gathered up the largest rocks I could find and threw them into the water, one by one. The bigger the splash, the better.

One day, an elderly man appeared seemingly out of nowhere. I was startled. He had been sitting on the opposite bank, but I hadn't noticed him. He walked in my direction, smiling, and with a friendly voice he said that I was welcome to be there, but the commotion I was making with the rocks disturbed him. He didn't actually tell me to stop, but that's what I heard. I had no idea who he was. I wondered if he knew me through my father, or whether I might be trespassing on his land. In that moment, however, the only thing that mattered was that he meant what he said; I heard him; and I stopped throwing the rocks.

You and I both know that there's nothing wrong with kids having a good time. The elderly man knew that too. I could see it in his eyes. I sat down to think about what had happened, and I remembered that when I was walking along the tracks earlier in the day, I had asked myself why I liked to make such a commotion in the water. It was just a passing thought, but as much as I liked to see those humongous splashes, they also reminded me of people who like to worry their dogs, stirring them up for no reason except to hear them bark. I never liked people who did that.

It wasn't until that evening, at home, that all the pieces fell into place. I realized that the pond was our dinner table. I loved them both. I loved to create disturbances now and again, *and* I loved the tranquility. Yet I had to face the fact that I had disturbed not only the elderly man, but also the pond, just like people who worry their dogs. At that point, I was no longer sure what the elderly man actually said to me, but I understood what the encounter with him meant: "Young man, can you remember the stillness? Do you know what it means?" Sitting at the dinner table, I wondered what kind of person I would grow up to be: someone who worries other people, just for the fun of it, or someone who understands a tranquil pool, and helps others to do the same?

I can feel your reaction: you're telling yourself that words like restful and peaceful—not to mention still, quiet, and tranquil—have no relation to anything that goes on at your dinner table, in your head, or anywhere else in your life. I doubt this is really the case, but I understand why you're thinking it. Nonetheless, if you're able to laugh—and I would bet you are—then you're closer to the stillness than you realize. My advice is to keep laughing until you turn the tables on those insatiable worries. I'm not trying to be funny, but how would you respond if you found real tranquility in your life? Would you feel at home? Or would you stir things up a little just to feel at home? *These are important questions on the spiritual path.* I know many good, hardworking, honest people who look for things to worry about—only because they're accustomed to worrying. Others I know like to make their friends worry because they have so much worry in themselves and so little trust in life. They're dissatisfied, I suppose, and they like to see others feel the same way. Although I'm not suggesting that you do these things, I want you to ask yourself how you use worry for your own unacknowledged purposes. That's what I mean by turning the tables on our worries, rather than letting them use you by controlling your life. The only way you can discover the truth is to find the stillness within yourself. I am certain that you can find it. You may not like everything you see, but that's okay. By doing this, you'll recover the trust in life that you may have lost over the years, and your soul will be very pleased.

One of the most sublime and beautiful of all Christian teachings actually addresses the fact of our worries, admitting to their presence, without saying that they are wrong. Jesus said:

> Therefore I tell you, do not worry about your life, what you will eat or what you will drink, or about your body, what you will wear. Is not life more than food, and the body more than clothing? Look at the birds of the air, they neither sow nor reap nor gather into barns, and yet your heavenly Father feeds them. Are you not of more value than they? And can any of you by worrying add a single hour to your span of life? And why do you worry about clothing? Consider the lilies of the field, how they grow; they neither toil nor spin, yet I tell you, even Solomon in all his glory was not clothed like one of these. But if God so clothes the grass of the field, which is alive today and tomorrow is thrown into the oven, will God not much more clothe you—you of little faith? Therefore, do not worry, saying, "What will we eat?" or "What will we drink?" or "What will we wear?" For it is the Gentiles who strive for all these things, and indeed your heavenly Father knows

that you need all these things. But strive first for the kingdom of
God and his righteousness, and all these things will be given to
you as well. So do not worry about tomorrow, for tomorrow will
bring worries of its own. Today's trouble is enough for today.

(MATTHEW 6:25–34, NRSV)

I can think of no other teaching that is more obvious and straight-forward, and yet so profoundly true, which is exactly why we're so prone to overlook or dismiss its meaning. Jesus acknowledges our worries, but he also draws a rather clear line: anything beyond "today's troubles" puts us on shaky ground, spiritually. We know that he's right, but we're not quite ready to put our trust in life or God. We tell ourselves that his words are too lofty or out-of-touch with the "real world" we know every day. And we are right—there are always good reasons to worry. And if we can't think of any right now, we'll do our level best to find some!

It was our worried conversation that led to this letter, particularly when we discussed the attack on the Twin Towers and all that has come after it. That was a horrible day. It was an act of murder that pushed everyone (or nearly so) beyond the line of trust. Almost immediately, countless people could be heard saying, "Now everything has changed." In reality, nothing could be further from the truth. The Ten Commandments, the Beatitudes, the Yoga Sutras, or the Eight-Fold Path—none of these changed. Nothing changed the essential teachings of the spiritual path. The part of us that would be content throwing rocks in a tranquil pool—or disturbing the dinner table, or worrying our dogs and our friends just to see them agitated—would be quite happy to believe that everything has, in fact, changed. That's what falling into the abyss feels like. I readily confess to worrying about terrorism, as well as the lilies, the birds, the rivers, and the climate. It's true: the world really is in terrible shape. These are today's troubles *and* tomorrow's. Yet God's Providence has not changed. The Spirit still weaves life through the whole creation. God's love has not changed. The transformative power of forgiveness has not changed. Jesus' teaching about worry has not changed.

That beautiful passage from the Bible is telling us to find the presence of God in the great body of life, and then strive to make that same presence known by the way we live. When I feel worried and stressed, I go outside for a long walk. Along the way, I search for a comfortable, secluded place. A still body of water is always good, but in lieu of that, I lie flat on the ground and give myself to the stillness. Nearly always my worries tell me that I have better things to do, but they're wrong. Instead, I find the silence within like a trusted old friend—like the one I met by the railroad tracks years ago. Then, I listen. I don't hear Jesus saying that he'll come to our rescue in worrisome times. I don't hear him promise to carry away the chosen few to a better and blissful place. I don't hear him say that greed is good, and it's okay to lose your trust in life. What I do hear him say is this: "Now I want you to get up, put your trust in me, and do something.... Today's troubles are enough, and they are very real indeed."

Faithfully yours.

18. BODY AND SPIRIT

My Dear Friend,

I would like to think that you've enjoyed this gorgeous weather. Maybe a trip to the mountains or the beach? If you haven't, then you still have a few weeks to make amends with your family. The summer months have been magnificent here, and I've enjoyed every available moment. I say that despite the aggravating tug-of-war I've had with this letter. The problem is the subject I'm writing about: the body, my body, the human body. You must be aware of the mistrust that much of the Christian tradition has directed toward the body, sometimes regarding it as an enemy on the spiritual path or the enemy's stronghold. Today, many people reject this view, and for good reasons: it adds insult to injury for those who don't like their bodies; it represents a decidedly bleak outlook on human existence; and it disregards the obvious fact that without our bodies we would be dead. My experience is that the body can be a terrible obstacle, *and* it can also be a spiritual gift—usually it is *both*, rather than one or the other.

The purpose of my letter is simply to explain why I'm saying this, but there's nothing very simple about it. The body is an extraordinarily important and complicated subject. It involves what we see with the naked eye, the physical world, and a great deal that we don't ordinarily see. Anyone who follows the spiritual path does so in *and* through their bodies. This seems obvious enough. My letter traces some notable parts of the journey that I've made in this regard: what I've learned this very week around the house, what I've learned over the years from reading the testimony of others, how that has helped me better understand my childhood, and finally, a lesson from an indigenous shaman who helped me begin to make sense of it all. The story seems circuitous—much more than it really is—but lives are like that: there's always more going on than we realize, and it involves our bodies more than we would ever believe. My hope is that you'll appreciate your body as the Holy Mystery that it's meant to be and perceive your whole self within the larger body of life that makes all our lives possible.

My difficulty with this letter has been the struggle to put my experience into words. In situations like this, a breakthrough often comes in a dream or out of the blue when I'm walking or thinking about something else. So, I slept and walked around a lot, waiting for the moment of insight to arrive. It was silly to do that, and I should've known it wouldn't work. I was acting on a version of the very assumption that I wanted to avoid: that *seemingly* disembodied experiences, like dreaming or unexpected flashes of intuition, are more "spiritual" than the ordinary routines of our lives every day. Finally, I realized that what I needed was some old-fashioned physical labor. Instead of ignoring my body, I decided to bring my whole self—body, mind, and spirit—into the process. The key was to move the subject out of my mind, where it was stuck, by working it through some blood, breath, bones, and muscles.

My solution was to rebuild a partially collapsed stone wall along the driveway leading to my house. You probably don't know this, but rebuilding an old stone wall is backbreaking work. Not only that, the hands and eyes of a skilled artist are required, neither of which I have. Nevertheless, the work I did on that wall was a creative act for me. There were moments of true revelation. I dug out a hundred or more large stones buried under soil formed from decayed and decaying leaves. Under some of those stones, I found three-hundred-million-year-old fossilized sea creatures, beautiful lichens that testify to an ancient history of their own, and multi-colored beetles that scurried away as soon as they saw me—not to mention a few snakes and several stinging bees that chased me away when I saw them. With a great deal of sweat pouring down my face, I imagined my predecessors who worked on this same wall, having many of the same thoughts and feeling the same sunshine with smiles on their faces too. The way I see it, rebuilding this stone wall was a profoundly spiritual experience, and it still is: Whole communities of living creatures were involved; they participated in the healing of my soul through the efforts of my body; and they helped me write the letter that you're holding in your hands now. Without their assistance and the work of my sore muscles, I would still be stuck in my head, not knowing what to say or how to say it. So I'm grateful to all these bodies, all the bodies of the earth, including mine.

Our bodies are anything but an enemy on the spiritual path, but I wouldn't dismiss the ancient traditions of the church just because they're old and seem out of touch with our lives today. Those early Christian saints and sages were amazing people, and they understood something that we need to know. Saint Anthony of Egypt, a towering spiritual figure in the third and fourth centuries, is a great example. For him, the body was not only an enemy, but a formidable one at that. He exerted great effort to discipline and restrain his body. I see no reason to mistrust his experience. I have to believe that he knew his body and himself better than anyone else—except God.

To understand Saint Anthony, you have to take into account the difference between "the body" and "the flesh," a distinction that Saint John, the gospel writer, also made: "It is the Spirit that gives life; the flesh is useless" (John 6:63, NRSV). Anthony's spiritual battles were with "the flesh." By that he meant those corrupted desires and passions that seem to enter into our bodies and shape who we think we are. We don't make distinctions like that today, and his real concern may have had very little connection to anything we consider the body to be. We think of our bodies in ways characteristic of our time: for instance, from a scientific or medical point of view, or as consumers who look into store windows and see mannequin-like figures that we adorn with clothes. Neither of these possibilities were part of Anthony's world. They wouldn't have occurred to him. Instead, he waged war against the flesh in his body, which may not occur to us. The irony is that when he turned his attention to the world around him, it was the flesh that he observed. He saw people who no longer appreciated the value of silence and always wanted more and more things. That's what he said nearly two thousand years ago, yet he could've been speaking about our time too. I honestly find his point of view to be more realistic and life-affirming than world-denying or body-hating. I can't say that I like his overall outlook on life, but I can understand why he followed the spiritual path in the way he did.

Saint Anthony seems to have nothing in common with Walt

Whitman, the great life-affirming poet whose writings I love. Their personalities are so different that it's almost laughable to include their names in the same sentence. Anthony sought refuge as a desert monk, which was as far from the city as he could get. Whitman was a New Yorker who celebrated the city, the countryside, and nearly everything he saw in American life. Whitman declared, rather boldly for his time, "I sing the body electric." That is the last thing that Saint Anthony would've said, ever, under any circumstances. It is possible that Anthony would have regarded Whitman as an egomaniac. Obviously, I don't know that for a fact. The only way we could know for sure is to ask them both. I would love the opportunity, but they're no longer here—not exactly. The spirit of their souls lives on in our hearts, while the molecules of their bodies recycle again and again in the great body of life.

I do know that Whitman loved life, *and* he gave of his life to help others. I'm thinking of his tireless work among wounded soldiers during the Civil War—people who suffered horribly, whose bodies had been blown to smithereens, and who knew that their wounds would likely lead to amputation. Whitman spent time with them, by the side of their beds, and he wrote letters to their families on their behalf. How many people do you know who would do the same? Very, very few. What I'm saying is that Whitman and Anthony followed the spiritual path in different ways; their words were different; and their worlds were worlds apart. Yet they were both keenly aware of human suffering and of the corruptible human soul. In their own ways, they both understood that the body is the temple of the Spirit. Anthony's life testifies to the terrible obstacle that the flesh can be on the spiritual path. He emphasized the Spirit over anything related to the body, because he knew how trapped we are in the flesh. Whitman, on the other hand, followed the spiritual path in his way, walked through the mystic's door, and celebrated the life he saw so abundantly around him.

Like I said, my experience is that the body is both an obstacle and a gift, so you can understand why I love Anthony *and* Whitman. If they were still with us, I can imagine both of them asking the very same question of us: How do we spend the greater part of our waking lives? The answer we would normally give is somewhere indoors, perhaps in front of a computer screen or television, which Saint Anthony would see as riddled with the flesh; and Whitman, as strangely electric, but disturbingly disembodied. I don't know that for a fact either, but if cyberspace is a new kind of "body" that we're creating, then my guess is that Anthony and Whitman would both say we have a lot to learn about its spiritual implications. I'm not against cyberspace, not any more than I'm against any kind of body, but my answer to their question is obvious: I would rather be on my front porch, where I can breathe easier and feel the warmth of the sunrise.

That's exactly what I'm doing this morning, and I'll tell you what it's like. The quiet is noticeable. I can hear only a few sounds in the distance: two dogs greeting each other about who knows what, a busy woodpecker, and my neighbor, Carol, training her rescued horses in their corral across the road. The rustling of leaves precedes the wind rising up the hill toward the house. Tree by tree, it approaches the front yard and the porch, where it touches my skin. I like the wind; I like my body; I like being in my body; I like everything about being here.

The sense of touch reminds me of the many rivers for which the Catskill Mountains are famous: the Beaverkill, Willowemoc, Rondout, Esopus, and Delaware. I love the rivers too, and their names, and the sound that water makes. I love the feel of water curling around my legs when I stand in it. All this changes how I perceive myself. The rivers and the wind tell me that "my body" is part of a larger body. Because they are part of me, these mountains, the rivers, and the wind are also "mine" to care for and enjoy—like my body. But ultimately, they're neither "mine" nor "ours," but God's. These are some of the many bodies of the one Spirit that sustains all life. My body, your body, Saint Anthony's body, and Whitman's body are all temples of the one Spirit.

The stillness of the early morning is especially good for meditation and prayer. To pray is to find the stillness within ourselves; and when we find it, certain sights and sounds, perceived through the senses, reveal the Spirit's presence. But on the spiritual path, it's the silence behind the stillness that we're looking for. Inner silence is the door to communion with God (which is Anthony's path) and with the great body of life that is God's (and this is Whitman's). Anthony was right about "the flesh." Our preoccupations, fears, and selfish desires create a great deal of noise in the temple of the body, so much noise that we no longer hear anything but the sound of the flesh. The flesh would like to have our attention all for itself. The flesh would have us believe that Anthony hated life, rather than affirmed it, and that Whitman's affirmation of life obscured the presence of God. The flesh has always been a deceiver.

Sitting here on my front porch, I realize that I've followed the spiritual path by bringing together those two seemingly conflicting views of life. I think of it in connection with the cave that a friend and I dug behind my childhood home. He lost interest after a few days, but I made it my home away from home—a Whitman-like celebration of life in the refuge of an Anthony-like cave. That cave became a sacred place of my very own. A natural spring flowed into a small brook only a few feet away. The brook meandered slowly through the remains of three old, shingled buildings that had once been a secluded neighborhood park. I would sit at the cave's entrance, or just inside, listening to the sound of the water winding through the valley. My body was part of the life around me, which meant that my body had not yet become an object in my mind. During those playful, simple, unstructured moments, I learned that the Mystery of life is our primary reality. That was when I first perceived the body as the temple of the Spirit. My life then was considerably more embodied and less fleshy than the version of reality we learn as adults.

I carried that memory with me, several years later, to Costa Rica, where I was doing summer work in anthropology with some fellow college students. We were traveling into a remote rain forest region known as Talamanca. Toward the beginning of the trip, I knew that the days ahead would be seriously important for me. I was a little afraid, and I knew some culture shock was involved, as well as fear. At the same time, I also knew that something more was going on. I just didn't know what it was. For nearly twenty-four hours, I separated myself from my friends. I didn't speak one word. Instead, I stayed put in my hammock, sleeping a little, but mainly remembering the inner silence I had known in my cave. Strangely—or not so strangely—when I woke up the next morning, I was completely refreshed and ready to move ahead.

A few weeks later, my friends and I were making a strenuous three-day hike into the higher elevations of the mountains. One night we stayed with a well-known Cabecar shaman who graciously allowed us to pitch our hammocks in and around his house. Late that evening, I stored away my clothes after dinner, and strung my hammock between two poles that supported the roof of his house. I heard the Rio Coen in the distance; and again, I lay there listening and remembering. I watched him walk to the front steps of the house, where he greeted a young man who approached from the forest edge. They spoke discreetly for a few minutes, apparently about a problem that needed a cure. Then, the visitor entered the house and sat quietly on a small stool only a few feet from my hammock. The shaman sang softly, as he walked back and forth between his private room and the open area where everyone gathered. Finally, he sat on his stool beside a small table. While all this was happening, I lay there quietly, listening to the river and the sound of his voice. When I finally looked at my watch, I saw that it was two in the morning—nearly three hours had passed.

I must ask you ahead of time to set aside any superstitious reactions you may have to the last part of my story. Don't think our generation or any generation simply leaves behind old fears and prejudices with the past. Superstition is wrapped up with culture and the psyche, but it is born of the flesh, rather than the Spirit. It stirs up just as much noise in our minds today as it did centuries ago, and we still make bad decisions because of it. Those same old fleshy enemies are still with us, which I was soon to learn firsthand.

After looking at my watch, my attention turned to the forest. It seemed so quiet, or so I thought. I listened more carefully and realized the forest was actually quite noisy in its distinctive way, and the sense of quiet was within me. Apart from the shaman's singing, no words were spoken by anyone, although a great deal was said through his eyes. When he first glanced in my direction, I didn't give it much thought; but after the second time, I knew instinctively that my relation to him had somehow changed. No longer was I observing him; rather, he was observing me, and I was participating in a way that I didn't understand.

From that point on, everything happened very quickly. When he looked at me a third time, our eyes met. I could see a bright light emanating from the area around his face. Instantly, in the moment I saw it, it enveloped me. For the next few seconds, all I could sense was a dense gray fog that surrounded me all around. At first, I felt a touch of panic, which immediately subsided. The possibility of evil intent crossed my mind too, but something deep within me knew that this was completely wrong. Instead, I heard myself thinking that the appearance of fog could be the awareness of my own disorientation, as strange as that sounds. In other words, I was witnessing my inability to comprehend anything about what was happening. Then, I remembered that I had seen the fog before. It was only a week or so earlier when I had lain in my hammock for nearly a day, and much earlier than that, all the way back to those times when I sat in my childhood cave. I wondered how many other times I had seen it, how many times we've all seen it, but dismissed it because we literally don't know what to make of it. The fog was the outer boundary of inner silence, and the place of crossing over to a very different experience of the world. Before I would always fall asleep when I saw it, but now I was very much awake.

As soon as I remembered all this, my awareness gravitated to the sound of the river in the distance, and hearing it carried me through the fog. Suddenly, I saw the forest through a light that was both within me and part of everything: the trees, the branches, the leaves, the whole forest canopy was laced with shimmering threads of radiant light. Tears flowed from my eyes—joyful tears—because I knew that the forest was alive with the presence of God. This was the shaman's gift. He helped me break through the fog, so I could see beyond the flesh: the Spirit weaving everything that exists, including you and me, into one body of light. It was not the forest that had changed—I had changed.

I can't explain all this in a way that fully satisfies my rational mind. For many years, I tried, but eventually I gave up. I don't worry about that anymore. But I often think of my cave by the stream, the shaman by the Rio Coen, and the light. I've never said much about it, but I often think of the radiant forest as the earth's spiritual body, and I ask myself what its relation to Christ's resurrected body might be. The web of life and the body of Christ are both part of the one Spirit. On two other occasions, I had similar experiences with holy people from very different traditions—one Christian, the other Hindu. They both had found the silence, each in their own ways. And their physical bodies, having become much less fleshy, radiated the same magnificent light—the so-called spiritual body that's mentioned, but not described, in the holy scriptures. All I really know is that I see the world very differently now. I know that there are many kinds of bodies, and we know so little about our own. I understand that it is *here*—in the here and now—that we live, die, and live again. I think of it when I'm baptizing someone in the church: the sound of the water pouring into the font is the same; the Spirit is the same; the human form before me is the same. I remember how mesmerized we are by the flesh, yet I also know that once the spell is broken, the promise of what our bodies are meant to be—temples of the Spirit—breaks through like a bright sunrise. That's why I want you to go outside, sweat a little, and enjoy the great outdoors. There's more going on than you realize—a great deal more.

Faithfully yours.

19. PERSEVERANCE

My Dear Friend,

It was great to hear from you. The chance to talk on the phone doesn't come often, so I'm always pleased when it does. I'm especially pleased to hear about the inner peace that's emerging in your life, but I'm a little surprised by the way you brought it up, almost as an afterthought toward the end of our conversation. You could have said more. I wish you had said more, but it's okay. I have to assume that you're testing the waters, cautious person that you are, which would explain your near-avoidance of the subject. Caution is wise, but having heard you say, on other occasions, that "nothing really good ever happens to me" (no doubt this is a gross exaggeration), I confess to wondering whether the same sentiment shapes your feelings about this. Perhaps you're doubting yourself, questioning this newfound inner peace too much, and wondering whether it might be an illusion or a passing mood.

I'm not holding you accountable for your feelings or even asking you to comment on them. I could be wrong—and I make no claim to knowledge of your innermost thoughts—but I really think you should ease up on yourself. My letter explains why I believe this. Just consider what I have to say without trying to fix something that isn't broken. I've known people who've begun to experience inner peace for the first time in their lives, and then worry themselves about it so much that it finally disappears. I don't want this to happen to you. My advice is to keep the caution, but let go of the doubt. It's okay to believe a little. Who knows—soon, probably very soon, when it finally dawns on you that the inner peace is real, you might believe quite a bit more.

There is no doubt in my mind that ordinary negative thoughts— like "nothing really good ever happens to me"—are some of the most tenacious obstacles you'll ever face on the spiritual path. Do you remember saying that? In the moment, they may seem harmless enough; but add them up, day after day, and you realize how destructive their impact can be. Basically, they wear you down through slow self-sabotage. This, perhaps more than any other time, is when perseverance is absolutely required. People usually think of perseverance as keeping a stiff upper lip through difficult times or plowing through really bad things that happen. It makes sense in situations when the obstacle is more tangible, but ordinary negative thoughts are not like that. The best thing you can do is to make small changes in your everyday habits, being deliberate as you go, while putting your faith in God. I'll give an example of what I mean by small changes, but I can't emphasize enough the part about faith. Persevere in faith too— that's what tradition teaches, and it's true. There is every reason to believe that your feeling of inner peace is real. Why shouldn't it be real? Trust it. Have some faith. You might be surprised.

Some of the best lessons I've learned on the spiritual path have come from Luke, my bluetick coonhound. I'm really quite serious, and I'm thinking of important, basic lessons—like perseverance—which are the hardest to learn. Some time ago, a wise friend told me that the greater part of spiritual growth takes place when we learn to live like a "good animal." I knew exactly what she meant; and now, through Luke, I understand it even better. Before telling you about Luke, I should make a few more comments about my friend. You can't really appreciate what she meant by thinking of "good" in customary moral or moralistic terms. She was speaking about spiritual common sense, which involves intuition. In other words, everyone knows what a "good animal" is like, in the same way that everyone knows that Luke is a good dog when they see him.

Also (I'm not really telling you about Luke yet, but I have to mention him—I love that dog), Luke would never make you think of the saying "It's a dog-eat-dog world." Sayings like that describe a hostile human world that has no relation to the world of a good dog. Asha, my wife, once told me that when she was a child, she misheard "It's a dog-eat-dog world," and believed that it meant "It's a doggy-dog world." I loved it. She was thinking of dogs and people as basically happy beings who like to eat, play, sleep, and find contentment doing whatever dogs and people like to do. It never occurred to her, not until much later in life, that anyone could have possibly meant anything else. She understood what a "good dog" is like, just like my friend understood what a "good animal" is like. Everyone knows. The question is whether we forget what we already know; and if we have, are we willing to persevere enough to remember?

Now I'll tell you about Luke. I was very proud when he completed his "Canine Good Citizen" course. He was enthusiastic about going to class; he made new friends very easily; and he was happy to learn new things. On the last day of the course, when all the dogs were evaluated, Luke received the best score for "separation anxiety," which means he has very little. This is significant because anxious dogs, like people, have a tendency to be overly cautious, wary, and troublesome. Often their frustration builds up to the point where it becomes outright aggression. They forget how to be good dogs. In that sense, they're very much like us. We get so stuck in our fears and frustrations that we forget how to do the most basic things: how to breathe properly, approach other people (and dogs) in a friendly manner, and care for others and ourselves. Basically, we forget how to live. A good dog hasn't forgotten how to live. A good dog hasn't forgotten how to be happy.

A large part of Luke's secret is that he frequently enacts an important piece of instinctive dog knowledge. It's a ritual of sorts— a superbly competent, canine version of yoga. Several times a day, but always in the early morning, he shakes the full length of his body in one continuous, intricate, and vigorous motion. He begins with the head, flapping his long ears against his scalp and jowls. Next, the full length of his backbone and legs becomes involved, until he completes this single movement with a flourish at the tip of his tail. Every bone and muscle, perhaps every cell, shakes and shimmies in this intricate action. That's how Luke prepares himself for the day, rather than thinking, for example, "Nothing really good ever happens to me," which is the kind of preparation people might make.

You have to admire Luke. He instinctively knows that the tail doesn't wag the dog. What he already knows but might forget, we must learn or we'll surely forget. My advice is to think of perseverance in much the same way. Rather than waking up in the morning to the thought of how bad things are—perhaps you imagine huge obstacles that you have to overcome by sheer determination, faith, and courage—just make up your own version of Luke's yogic dance. Maybe you should take some yoga classes and develop your own morning routine. If not, then at least you can sing in the shower. Whatever you decide, make it a daily habit. I'm not kidding. That's what perseverance through the small, but really difficult obstacles looks like.

The very first sign of resistance on your part will be the idea that negative thoughts can be shaken off so easily—in the manner of Luke. You're probably telling yourself that people are very different from dogs, or from any kind of animal, and you're right. Frankly, I don't believe Luke has negative, self-sabotaging thoughts. Am I supposed to say that this makes him less than human? It's better to say, "God bless him," and follow his lead (pun intended), than to interpret what he already knows and does so well as a reason to refuse to learn it yourself.

The fact is that you've already persevered quite admirably— creating space in your life for something new, taking time to sort things out, praying and meditating, getting plenty of exercise. But now, something new is beginning to emerge. My guess is that it's even greater than you would believe—were you to try actually believing. Perhaps this sense of inner peace will lead to a deeper experience of love, and perhaps you have some fear of that possibility. In any event, the next step is to become familiar with this mysterious unknown in your life. Be cautious all you want; persevere by testing the waters; but don't turn away now or run away, when the door you've been looking for has finally begun to open. Shake off those negative thoughts. It's just that easy and just that simple. You can trust Luke. He knows what's he's doing. He's learned it through millions of years of dog evolution; and we've learned through human evolution that if we're unwilling to learn some new habits, one day at a time, then we most definitely won't learn them. That's what I mean by perseverance.

On several occasions, I've encouraged you to see the different parts of your inner life as friends, or as strangers who could become friends, or as unfriendly types that masquerade as friends. Now, let me make two additional suggestions along the same lines. First, think of this new sense of inner peace as a long-lost friend. The fact that it's emerging at this time in your life does not necessarily mean you haven't known it before. Maybe you've just forgotten, or you never considered yourself worthy. Maybe you've pushed it away in the past, possibly more than once. Now, you're being given another chance. There will be some nervous anticipation on your part— some concern that the reunion might not turn out well. You might even consider making up an excuse about your whereabouts, hoping to reschedule this fateful meeting for a later time. I'm suggesting that now is the time to shake off the past—anything that would make you believe "Nothing good ever happens to me." Give yourself permission to trust the inner peace for what it is. Inner peace is real. Love is real. And, by all means, attend your reunion. What greater purpose does it serve to say, "Nothing good ever happens to me," when it so clearly has? Just show up, and be friendly. Luke knows what I'm talking about, and so do you.

Second, learn to claim this inner peace as your own, while realizing that "it" is not an "object" that can be "owned" or used like a personal possession. Exactly the same principle applies to all our relationships. We don't own each other. We don't own God. Shake off any thoughts you may have that love can be "had" or "controlled" in this way, and give yourself permission to feel more settled and at ease with yourself. I would bet that there's some separation anxi-ety going on in your own life—between you and God—and now the opportunity has come for you to feel at home again. There's no reason to be afraid. God has never abandoned you.

I hope you will seriously consider what I'm saying. The Spirit has been drawing you out from your hiding place for some time. You've responded well and persevered through a great deal of turmoil and confusion. But there is more: the Spirit has announced a personal, face-to-face meeting. The sense of inner peace emerging in your life is the invitation. You could avoid it altogether, choosing to cut and run. I hope you will not do this. I know you're nervous, and I know you don't understand everything that's going on. But you're not supposed to have all the answers. You're not supposed to know everything that will happen or might happen. Tradition and expe-rience tell us that the peace of God is "beyond understanding"—which is the reason I want you to appreciate the great Mystery at work in your life and accept it for what it is. This is the gift we've all been given, but have difficulty receiving. Just persevere enough to show up. That's really all you have to do. Luke teaches me this les-son every day, and he knows what he's doing.

Faithfully yours.

P.S. Don't forget to sing in the shower—and it doesn't matter if you can't sing!

20. THE FAMILY

My Dear Friend,

For several weeks, my life has been completely swamped by pastoral work, one family crisis after another, and I've had precious little time for anything else. Now, having finally read your letter, it appears that you've been dealing with essentially the same issues: trouble at home and a great deal of disillusionment. You didn't put it quite that way, not in so many words, but it was easy enough to piece it together from the bits you gave me.

My impression is that it all started in the kitchen. The first "volley" (that's your word) came "seemingly" (that's my word) out of nowhere—"There must be more to life than this." You were astounded by the anger, yet its power was clear and undeniable. In a slightly different circumstance, it could have been a scream. What you heard was a lifetime of dreams and promises thrown out with the garbage. You felt wounded, so you retaliated by firing back nearly the same words yourself: "And there's definitely more to life than listening to this." An eye for an eye was your answer, which did nothing except add insult to injury. Both of you managed to say so much *and* so little; while the children, who heard everything, stood there, motionless, spellbound, and afraid. The youngest ran away, crying. You knew that you reacted badly, but it all happend so fast. Since then, the atmosphere at home has been polite and functional, which you regard as the calm before the storm.

You asked if we might discuss all this on the phone. I assume you want a sounding board or an ally. I really do understand your feelings; however, I must respectfully decline. It would be exceedingly unwise for me to counsel you about *your* family after hearing only *your* side of the story. Actually, I don't need to hear the details. I'm willing to offer a few comments on how your troubles at home relate to the spiritual path, and I'll go so far as to make some practical suggestions. But my real purpose is to impress upon you that "occasional" disillusionment in your family should not be taken lightly. Disillusionment with the way things are, if it is not addressed, can lead to something much worse. I'm talking about disenchantment with life itself. This is serious business. Rather than talking with me, my advice is to find out what your beloved actually means. Why? *Because there is more to life, a great deal more.* You, of all people, should appreciate the truth behind those words. You may bristle at the fact that someone said this to you. You may not like the tone with which it was spoken. But what difference does that make? None. You hear a door slamming in your face. I hear a door opening—and an invitation. The only thing that matters now is whether you're willing to see beyond your bruised ego, walk through that door, and take your whole family with you. If not, then maybe they'll take the initiative and carry you along until you finally wake up. Either way, the door has opened.

There is one more thing: I hope you don't expect me to tell you what the ideal family *should* look like or how people in your family *should* behave. If so, then you've definitely found the wrong person.

Despite the emphasis that the church customarily places on this, an image of "the family" is not something I think about very much or promote. The many healthy, happy, and spiritually grounded families that I know have different forms and arrangements. In my view, they're all sacred, and they all work quite well—even through the rough spots. Structure and stability are hugely important, and there's no question about the crucial ingredient: it's the love they have for each other, rather than an image of "the family" that they try to conform to. I'll say it again: it's the spiritual substance that matters the most, the love, rather than the outward form. Don't waste your time trying to defend yourself. Instead, defend them—the flesh and blood people who *are* your family—by taking them seriously. If changes in how your family works need to be made—in how you talk, work, play, and live—then by all means make those changes. You don't need my advice to do this, and you definitely don't need my permission. All you need to do is work it out with them—together.

My experience is that families that work well are gardens of the soul. Does that sound dreamy or ridiculous? Perhaps you also believe that "there must be more to life" sounds ridiculous? I am serious; and it's not the biblical garden that I have in mind, where the serpent is held accountable and women take the fall, but real, living gardens with soil that must be cared for so flowers and food can grow. This is a very basic and simple image. I like it because it turns our attention toward life's spiritual ground, which is an advisable place to start when someone close to your heart calls the meaning of life into question. And I commend it for another reason: it reminds us that families are not meant to be extensions of the television or the shopping mall. Perhaps this goes without saying, but people are not buying machines. We are not things. We're not inert objects that dress up well, but say little and think even less. We are not interchangeable or replaceable. And you, my friend, you can't go out and buy new families and friends like clothes and cars, although I have known some lunatics (that's my opinion) who have done exactly that.

Families are gardens of the soul because they teach us the sound of our names, good manners, how to speak and tie our shoes, how to take care of ourselves, and the meaning of love. Families shape who we are and how we feel about ourselves and life. Every newborn is a testimony to this simple truth: families depend entirely on the only real gifts we ever have to give—love, trust, commitment, honesty, joy, and forgiveness. All these gifts are completely sacrosanct and as essential to life as sunlight, rain, and good soil.

I would argue that the spiritual purpose of families is to nurture a deep sense of enchantment with life as a basic survival skill. By "enchantment," I mean a feel for the Mystery and joy of life through the love we have for each other. It all begins at home. The Mystery that exists out there corresponds with the Mystery within us. The irony is that the spiritual significance of enchantment turns our usual assumption on its head: to be enchanted does not involve falling under the power of a wicked spell. Joy and wonder provide a reliable, respectful, and clear-minded vision of life's meaning. It's disenchantment with life that casts a shadow over the soul, and it's disenchantment that you should be concerned about. There's nothing normal, ordinary, predictable, or well-behaved about this, just as there's nothing normal or ordinary about a newborn, or any part of the world, or God. You can see the joy of life in a person's eyes. It's elusive—you can't really explain it, but you can't explain it away, either.

I readily admit that it's quite easy to find any number of good, entirely rational reasons *not* to feel joyful, awestruck, and enchanted, the principal reason being the accumulated toll that living every day exacts on the soul: never-ending problems, emotional entanglements and misunderstandings, and the struggle to make ends meet, not to mention an exhausting daily routine. Life is good, but life is also overwhelming, which is part of the Mystery too. Consider the example of your own life. You freely accept your duties and responsibilities; from the bottom of your heart, you want to fulfill them. You are a responsible, hardworking person. *And* you are overwhelmed, so much so that your shared hopes and dreams seem increasingly out of reach as the years go by. There is no one to blame. This is no one's fault—this is life, and you and your family, together, must come to terms with it.

The good news is that the troubles you're having at home have not reached the point of disenchantment with life as a whole. What you're experiencing is disillusionment with the way things are. The problem is that unless you do something about disillusionment when it arises, then it will build, one brick after another, until all of you lose sight of the Mystery. That's why I'm advising you to take those words seriously—"There must be more to life." If you ignore them, then I can assure you that the following will happen: lovers will become enemies, friends will become strangers, and you and your loved ones will eventually find yourselves uprooted from the spiritual ground of your life together. I see it happen again and again, and I have no intention of mincing words about it now. Do not blame anyone, point your fingers, or even pretend to run away. Otherwise, your family will begin to resemble a hall of mirrors, rather than the garden it is meant to be.

So, what does all this mean? First, you need to understand that disillusionment may be emotionally painful, but on the spiritual path it is both necessary and good. Why? Because disillusionment is a step toward seeing beyond the hall of mirrors that we too often accept as "normal." For your sake and your family's sake, you must take that step. Your ego may be bruised. Like everyone, you have your shortcomings. You've made your share of mistakes. But a bruised ego is a small price to pay when loved ones tell you, perhaps screaming, that they want to remember the joy of life. That's what they want, and it's what you want. And think of your children. Not long ago, you told me about their questions at the dinner table: Is the North Pole really melting? Is everything going to be okay? The world they hear about in the news calls into question *their* future in ways that you can hardly imagine. They're young now, but soon they'll put the same question in another way: Why bother with today if tomorrow is in so much doubt? In their world, the distance between disillusionment and disenchantment is not very far. You've got your work cut out for you. So do we all.

I'm telling you this as a true spiritual friend: return to those incredibly well-chosen words, "There must be more to life," and find out what they mean. Talk about it; and when you do, set aside all those images and ideas about how your lives *should* be. Instead, talk about the way things really are. There's nothing more disillusioning and disenchanting than to hear people say things they don't really believe or to pretend to believe things that aren't really true. Neither you nor I have all the answers, and you don't need to be afraid of letting your family know that. My guess is that they know it already! So just be yourself. It's you that they love, not their image of you—and even less the image you have of yourself. Be honest about your feelings. By hiding behind your anxiety and fear, you create the impression in their minds that *any* problem in life has the power to disrupt or shatter the world you create together, which generates even more anxiety in them. Instead of looking to you for genuine hope and direction in life, they'll be waiting for the next shoe to drop, and that is a sure recipe for making life unbearable.

Some things are worth fighting for, and your family is one of them. I can't think of anything that dispels disillusionment better than a clear-minded person who believes in the power of love. This is your responsibility, but it's also an imperative of life and a basic survival skill that everyone in your family needs to learn. Disillusionment with the way things are can make people feel cynical about love; disenchantment with life distorts the meaning of love altogether. What you need to understand now is that love doesn't come out of nowhere. It doesn't come from the shopping mall, not any more than food comes from the supermarket. Your responsibility is to take care of the garden, and the garden that you've been given is your family. You can't be passive. You can't run away or throw it all away. Someone must till the soil, and that person is you.

I realize that all this is easier said than done. Your family needs transformation right now, and the only place to begin is with yourself. You must want transformation to happen. You must want it passionately, and know that you want it. This alone can be a huge step on the spiritual path. Do you want transformation enough to let go of your fear? Do you want it badly enough to resist finding fault with others and holding them accountable for your disillusionment? I'm thinking of the excuses we give: too much work and not enough money, or too much money and not enough work. Feelings of being taken for granted, taken advantage of, manipulated, overlooked, or ignored are possibilities too. Any or all of these feelings may be entirely justified, *and* they may build up, even to the point where your whole family might collapse under their weight. But I'm not asking you to like what you dislike or to be complicit with anything offensive, displeasing, or harmful. Questions about who is right and wrong have their place, very definitely, but real transformative change does not begin there. It begins when we're willing to call down the Spirit into the shadows we create for ourselves. I'll say it again: love does not come out of nowhere, and your spiritual journey is the life you already have.

In those difficult moments when you want to run or throw it all away, I want you to do something a little unusual. Why not? It doesn't hurt to break the mold now and again. If it's possible, I want you to go outside. Take a member of your family or the whole family, and build a small campfire. If you can't do that, then find a quiet room at home and light a candle. The important part is the flame, which represents the love that exists within you and your family. The flame you see is just as real as the one that burns in all of you. Then, I want you to do three things. First, call upon the presence of God. All you have to do is say it: "God, be with us." It's best to say it out loud, and be as clear as possible about your intent: *You want transformation in your life; you want to walk through that door.* You know that it's true, so for Christ's sake, say it.

Remember the bruised ego, the frustration and blaming, the discontent, and especially those utterly selfish moments you would rather forget. Then, put these thoughts in the flame: outdoors, write it all on a slip of paper and place it in the flame; indoors, just let your thoughts do the work for you. This will be your offering and your prayer. When someone laughs or suggests that this might be a little odd or crazy, which will surely happen, then think of the alternative: you could take them shopping in the hope that a few dollars will heal the rift among you. You would be telling them—and teaching them—that food really does come from the store, and love, from the pocketbook. Like I said, these days the distance between disillusionment and disenchantment is not very far, so don't go down that road.

These are your choices: either the hall of mirrors, or the garden of the soul; a trip to the mall, or spiritual transformation; an image of you that you want them to believe, or the real you. So which is it going to be?

Faithfully yours.

21. LIVELIHOOD AND CAREER

My Dear Friend,

I've been away for nearly a week, and it was only this morning that I heard your phone message. The possible career change sounds like good news, although the hurried tone in your voice gave it a slightly ambiguous spin. Would it be premature to say congratulations? I suppose it would, but I'll say it anyway because the opportunity you've been given is so well-deserved. I realize that the time you have to make this decision is unavoidably short, but it should be enough. I'm especially pleased to know of the support from your family and friends; and, I believe, you would like a similar vote from me. I really shouldn't make comments along those lines; however, I can say that I'm fully confident in your ability to make a wise decision.

I might also add that any change in a person's work, even under the most favorable circumstances, is usually quite stressful. I'm sure this is the case for you now. Boundaries become confused, and people often seek advice in not the best places. You need to remember that I'm no career counselor. My advice is to do your best to keep your own boundaries as clear as possible; otherwise, unnecessary and unfortunate complications can easily develop. So, let me stay within my role as your spiritual friend and make some comments on how changes in work can relate to the spiritual path.

There is no question about the significance of this decision. To find the right kind of work can thoroughly transform a person's life. Spiritual well-being is tied as much to our work as to any other part of our lives. I learned this when I left the classroom and became a priest. I believe I've mentioned this before, but from a slightly different angle. I loved teaching, and I loved anthropology. But standing before my students, I gradually realized that my "voice" as a person was better suited to the priesthood. Nevertheless, I could have remained in anthropology and thrived. Contrary to some prevailing opinions, religion has no monopoly on spirituality. Anthropologists and other scientists are some of the most ethical people I know. Deep spiritual truths are often revealed by understanding cultures different from our own. My decision was difficult, but I knew it was right; and once the decision was made, my life transformed in the most profound ways: how I related to other people, my sleep, my breathing, my appetite, my overall state of health. The change was profound enough to qualify as a spiritual event. My life improved by the fact of making a difficult decision.

I realize that fair compensation weighs heavily on your mind. This is definitely a moral issue. The financial risks involved with the new job may make you feel less secure, financially, but they seem manageable. Whatever decision you eventually make, now is the time to step back and consider the larger picture, and especially the often murky ideas our society has about work. As you put it, "meaningful work" or "livelihood" means having the opportunity to make a positive contribution to the community, while providing for the needs of your family. I completely agree, and would like to add that there are many ways to make a valuable contribution to the community. Where are the people who can fix my roof, or build a substantial piece of furniture, or make anything that anyone really needs? Fewer and fewer people can do these important things. At the same time, the spiritual significance of livelihood has lost ground in the face of meeting basic survival needs. Increasingly, people live on or near the margins of society, including the so-called middle class, whatever that means these days. Apparently, the majority feel helpless about this, believing that nothing can or should be done. To make matters worse, most of the churches have adopted this same stance, for the most part, positioning themselves quietly on the sidelines of any serious ethical discussion about the workplace.

I know that you've raised similar questions and concerns, and I hope your decision will take these considerations into account. "My" spiritual path, "my" work, "my" livelihood, and "my" career are important, but none of this is really viable apart from our lives together. An idiom of personal fulfillment shapes every part of our lives today, even to the point of making the pursuit of career goals a spiritual path in itself. The ancient "ladder of heavenly ascent" has been replaced by climbing the rungs of economic success. You would think the Spirit prefers to live in the higher regions of personal fulfillment called "a successful career," and would like to take us there as quickly as possible. Even if this was a genuine path— which it's not—very few people have the opportunity to climb it. A vital link to the sacred is severed when we separate personal fulfillment from livelihood and community. Spiritual values are subsumed by the marketplace, instead of being honored and celebrated. Communities unravel, rather than thrive; and the gifts we've been given in God's creation are consumed, instead of replenished. And people think the younger generation are the ones who need values clarification!

I know you have serious questions about the meaning of your work now. I'm not asking you to solve the problems of the world before reaching a decision, or to make the solution to those problems your new job description. I only hope you realize that the years of loyal dedication given to your current job and all the effort that's gone into providing for your family deserve great respect and admiration. You have already made a huge difference to your family and friends. Yet a crossroads has clearly been reached. The last several months of struggle with the Spirit have been exactly that—a struggle—and your work is one part of it. Now, your sincere desire for "the Spirit to be part of your life every day" is very real, and you should give it a high priority. If you like the language of "goals," then this one is achievable. You can reach this goal whether you stay where you are—rethinking your present commitments and the use of your income—or you take this new opportunity to make a change.

Here's my point: the issue is not really the career, but what you do with it. To make the Spirit part of your life every day is the purpose of the spiritual path. What you need is the right vehicle to make this happen. Tradition says that faith is everything we need, which is true. But we also need an understanding of how faith can be put into practice. I want you to consider this question: Do you believe that a new career will be the vehicle you're looking for? It may, in fact, be part of the answer. This is entirely possible. But I'm asking you to be practical about this from a spiritual point of view. What does your soul want you to do? Maybe the soul doesn't seem so relevant in our day and age. Maybe, as a people, we don't know what to think about the soul anymore. Maybe we're willing to believe in the soul as a possibility, but our words seem empty of conviction and faith. But it is the soul, rather than a new job, that carries us along the spiritual path. Jobs change, careers change, but your soul is "you."

Let me put this another way: Can you show me the soul on your résumé? No, but we both know what a life filled with soul looks like, as well as the vacant look in the eyes of anyone who has lost contact with his or her own. If you are looking for a more spiritually meaningful life, then consider the soul to be your prize. It cannot be reinvented like an image of "you" manufactured for a job interview. And the soul is not an appendix of the self, with a purpose so uncertain that it might be considered useless. I do know this: we weave magnificent souls when we give for the sake of giving, when we work for the love of our families and communities, and when the love of God and life radiates from the ordinary words we speak every day. We weave souls of beauty from the invisible inside of life—with the desires and dreams that rise up within us. The soul is a work of art in every person, a living record of where we have been and who we are becoming. I'll say it again: it's the soul, filled with the light of God, that carries us along the path.

When Christ says, "It is easier for a camel to go through the eye of a needle than for someone who is rich to enter the kingdom of God" (Mark 10:25), he's obviously talking about something beyond wealth. I don't want to be preachy, but this applies even to the riches in your resume, great as they are. Without question, your work has been excellent. However, the résumé and the career are the outer surface of your life, and now it's the inner meaning that you must take into account. Whether we are bricklayers or stockbrokers, parents, protesters, or priests, we cannot pass through the eye of the needle holding a résumé in our hands. As important as it may be (which I hope you realize), I don't think God will ask to see it.

I wonder about the sense of urgency in your message, and whether it remains in your voice even now. Our lives always move too fast. We make decisions too fast. But you can slow down within yourself, walking the spiritual path like a true pilgrim, and still meet your deadline. The world out there will not go away. Set aside a few quiet minutes. Imagine your soul as a character reference of sorts, speaking to God on your behalf. God asks your soul, "Who is this person?" My hope is that you will give yourself time to listen for an answer. Listen long enough for the invisible inside of life to speak through yours. The spiritual path requires time—each and every eternal moment that fills a lifetime. Apparently, in this present moment you are being called to awaken to some deeper truths.

Faithfully yours.

22. SOUL MEDICINE

My Dear Friend,

You've made a good decision, and I'm pleased with the way you made it. Any anxiety that you have will surely evaporate once you've grown accustomed to the new job and people in your life. I also appreciate your comments on my last letter, which I'm surprised you've had time to read in the midst of such a rapid transition. By the way, this is not the first time someone has asked, "Do you really believe in the soul?" It's a peculiar but good question to ask a priest—somewhat like asking whether I believe in God! My answer, of course, is "yes" on both counts. But I wonder what the impact would be if I said anything else: Would your faith become any less faithful; your hope, less hopeful? Possibly, but I hope not.

I understand the strange predicament you face. After struggling so long to find God and a path to follow, you return to the church and see very little interest in the soul. And when you actually find some interest, it usually takes the form of speculation or debate. For the most part, scientists and theologians are concerned with "the mind" these days—as a function of the brain—rather than the mind as an expression of "the soul." Both views have merit, but the reasons behind them are quite different. Scientists regard the soul, or the belief in it, as too mystical and imprecise for serious study. Large segments of the church have much the same opinion. They believe that too much emphasis on the soul gives us one more reason to ignore our moral responsibilities in the here and now. Actually, this makes a great deal of sense, and I tend to agree, at least to some extent. The Christian path, after all, is rooted in the incarnation of Christ—his flesh and blood existence and ours—which means we must never turn our backs on the suffering in this world, as tempting as it may be.

I see absolutely nothing wrong with thinking in terms of "the mind" and human consciousness, yet something truly significant seems to be missing in the contemporary outlook. If the soul has become a figure of speech or a figment of the imagination—which is to say, a fantasy—then why bother to search for it by scientific means? On the other hand, construing "the soul" as a possible "fact"—as scientists consider "facts" to be—will not make it any easier to find. None of this is news. Every schoolchild knows, or should know, that the Age of Reason surpassed the Age of Faith long ago. This is an obvious "fact" of history, which I tend to like. I was trained as a scientist and admire the honesty and courage it requires. The spiritual path calls for qualities that are very much the same.

Nevertheless, I would be cautious about glorifying either science or religion too much. Common sense alone suggests that the supposedly "religious" past was less faithful than we might assume; and our day, not so rational. Science is not your adversary as a follower of the spiritual path—nor is it the enemy of faith. It is true that science can be put to shadowy purposes, but the same can be said for religion and the church. The last thing I want to see is a religious attack on science or legislation proclaiming what must be taught in the classroom. This only adds chaos to the confusion, and I find it difficult to understand how a closed mind does anything to glorify God or humankind.

That is why I hope you will not be preoccupied with polarized debates between science and religion. The spiritual path calls out faith *and* reason. My advice is to use your intuition about this, while reflecting on the kind of "knowledge" or "evidence" for the soul that you would like to see. Let's imagine a team of hard-nosed scientists and devout theologians working together (this might stretch the imagination a bit), and they actually discover factual evidence for the soul's existence. What do you think would happen? Would the spiritual artifact be placed in a museum, along with the moon rocks and Lindbergh's plane? Or would a church be more suitable? I am being facetious on both counts. The idea of a church becoming a museum makes my skin crawl. Either way, the media would probably conduct extensive interviews with religious leaders and scientists. Both would feel vindicated—the church, for its traditional belief in the realm of the Spirit; and the scientists, for the faith they have in objective methods.

But really. Would this discovery make any difference to you and me personally? Would it take us any further along the spiritual path? The "fact" is that we don't know our hearts very well, and when we set out to discover sacred knowledge or evidence for spiritual "things," it is likely that whatever we find will become a trophy. It's the same with mystical experiences. Once they become "things"—objectified experiences stored away in our minds—then the ego takes over and their meaning is lost.

I honestly don't think this is the kind of knowledge you want, and besides, what we need is medicine—real, genuine, sacred medicine for the soul. Then we might be in a much better position to find the answer to your question. It would be easy simply to say that your faith is your soul medicine, but I think the better question is this: What are you going to do with your newfound faith? Do you see the difference?

I have been reflecting about this—and about you—late in the evenings, standing, as I often do, in my front yard, gazing at the stars. I like to watch their almost imperceptible movement across the sky. It settles the mind and slows my stream of thought to a pace much closer to the soul's. Although my grandmother was not a star-gazer herself, she was the one who helped me understand just how good this medicine is for me. Her soul medicine was teaching Sunday School and gardening, and she was immensely pleased when I joined her by the fireplace to study the Bible as she prepared her lessons. I enjoyed her company too, and learned a great deal.

I also found it very difficult to sit in her living room for very long. My great-grandfather's body was laid out in his casket there on the afternoon of his funeral. I always remember that. He was a wonderful man. He never said very much, and his reputation as a sometimes cranky old codger was widely known. People loved him for it though. The light in his eyes was pure gold, and I miss him terribly. So, after sitting with my grandmother for a while by the fire, I would usually go outside to watch the lightning bugs and the stars. She knew I liked my alone time. Once, and only once, she walked onto the porch a few feet from where I was standing. She saw me looking at the nighttime sky, and said, "Maybe the stars are souls on their way to heaven." I wondered if she was thinking of my great-grandfather, and when I saw her smile back at me, I knew she understood what I was thinking about. It was a moment of grace, which, by the way, was her name. Then, she returned to the fireplace, her Bible, and the lessons for Sunday. In those few words, she wasn't talking about the soul in any direct way, certainly not as a well-defined object of thought. And she wasn't really talking about my great-grandfather or the stars. Yet all these entered into her meaning, which, like her life, was deeply rooted in the spiritual path.

I know how easy it would be to see her comment as a quaint remnant of bygone days, a kind of folklore, I suppose. That would be the equivalent of putting her beliefs in a museum, dismissing their significance, without paying appropriate respect to the dead. My grandmother didn't know much about science. She did know about my interest in the Big Bang and every living creature I could find, but I never heard her express dislike for it. She lived in an out-of-the-way place you have never heard of and would never plan to visit. She was the last person on earth you would call "extreme." When she looked at the stars, she saw "the heavens," not a battlefield between religion and science, just as her garden was a few acres of God's good earth.

Perhaps what you need to understand is that my grandmother had little concern for buying, having, and owning things. It is very easy to get lost in a world of things. We even imagine the self as an "object" that can be manufactured and reconstituted for one purpose or another. What a dreadful idea. Perhaps that's the reason we have so much trouble imagining the soul and talking about its meaning, which is life's meaning. We've lost the words; and with the words, the reality they stand for.

Around the fireplace, she spoke about the "kingdom of God" and the "resurrection." That was the core of her faith. In a different moment, outdoors, under the nighttime sky, she said, "Maybe the stars are souls on their way to heaven." She was letting me know that the fire in the fireplace, the flame in our hearts, the starlight and the fireflies, the light in her eyes, in the eyes of my ancestors, and in yours and mine are all reflections of the one true Light. These are lesser lights, to be sure, but they are living signs of life's inner meaning. This was my grandmother being faithful to her faith. She wanted me to always remember the spiritual journey, especially given the likely event that I would lose my way. We all do at one time or another. She wanted me to remember that we come from God into this world, and here we are given the opportunity to learn how to live in the presence of God's love. Finally, someday, we all make the ultimate passage and return to God.

I can also imagine something else that happened. While I was outside, she was in the living room, reading her Bible, praying. Call it whatever you want—intuition, insight, love—but the Spirit led her to her grandson, and the Spirit put the right words in her mouth. What I really want you to understand is that her words were a blessing. A blessing is an empowering and exceptionally sacred gift that anyone can give. Blessings are real, just as the soul is real, and God is real. They have absolutely no relation to a world constituted by "things." Blessings happen through the Spirit who calls out the light of God within us. The Spirit gives us the opportunity to receive its blessing and share it with others. Blessings are soul medicine. They affirm the spiritual fact that our lives matter, that we have a right to exist, and that we live in a world filled with Spirit. I believe this is the evidence for the soul that you're looking for. We couldn't put it in a museum if we tried.

My suggestion is simply to pray as my grandmother did. Pray

with an open mind and learn the sacred art of blessing the people in your life. Bless your food at mealtime, and the trees, the stars, the fireflies, and everything you see. Life has an inner form and purpose, and ours is to become vessels of grace—living souls—pouring out the love of God in our lives every day. Be well, my friend.

Faithfully yours.

23. STAYING AWAKE

My Dear Friend,

I have no doubt about your desire and enthusiasm for following the spiritual path. I've known it all along; it is clearly evident in your last letter; and I want to affirm it. Yet I say this knowing that affirming comments must be made carefully between spiritual friends. Affirmation is good when it fosters a clear-headed faith, particularly at times when we might otherwise give up. The problem is that we can become dependent on affirmation, enslaved to potentially misleading or false ideas about ourselves, including the illusion that we're ready to go further and faster on the spiritual path than is either desirable or possible. One of our most difficult challenges is simply to stay awake once we've taken up the path. In that regard, the affirmation that you apparently want from me may be the last thing you really need! I can't think of anything that's more likely to put us back to sleep than hearing affirming comments from our friends.

I'm bringing this to your attention because of your desire "to move ahead," as your letter so clearly stated. I do not want to dampen your spirit, but you must understand that spiritual awakening is a gradual process that cannot be speeded up—despite your enthusiasm. Everyone has illusions and delusions about themselves. To ignore or deny this humbling fact is a sure sign of trouble ahead. For that reason, I think it's time to examine the intent behind your letter, which involves taking responsibility for yourself more thoroughly than you would like at this moment. This is, in fact, what "moving ahead" often looks like.

I want to share a story about an important relationship I once had with a teacher. The circumstances are very different from yours, but the underlying issue is very much the same. I was fortunate to have had many good teachers; and one, who taught history, took a real interest in all his students, including me. He noticed that I sometimes seemed to withdraw during his lectures. He told me so. He was right. I often peered out the large clear windows in the classroom, so much so that he finally questioned me about it, asking whether I was daydreaming or asleep. In a sense, I was both asleep and daydreaming, but I was paying attention too. The class was captivating. His description of events in history carried my imagination away—seemingly out the window—when, in fact, I was hearing every word. I told him the truth, and he believed me, which was an important kind of affirmation in itself. It gave me confidence in him as a person because I knew he was taking me seriously. I loved his lectures; I looked up to him; and I wanted him to think highly of me.

Yet, in truth, I was struggling with the class. For whatever reason, I had a difficult time understanding this one particular period of history, nineteenth-century Europe. The facts were easy to learn, and I learned them. But secretly, I felt uncertain and insecure. I couldn't relate, personally, to anything that was being said. By learning the facts, I was covering up my secret. When he asked how I felt about the subject, I told him how well I was doing and how much I liked it. My grades suggested that this was the case. So, I hid the truth, while refusing to ask for help of any kind, simply because I wanted to maintain a favorable impression.

Eventually, he broke the ice. He knew all along what was going on, and he confronted me: "Jeff, I know you're a good student. But if you refuse to let people help you, then you won't be able to learn what you want to know." I was mortified, and yet I knew he was right, and so did he. After that, I always asked for help when I needed it—well, almost always. My point is that he was teaching me that the spiritual path is not about trying to please others, but taking responsibility for the truth of one's own life.

I want you to understand that constant enthusiasm is no more a precondition of our friendship than my affirmation of you as a person. It would be natural to assume this, believing that it's necessary to create a favorable image in my mind, especially when you may feel very differently about yourself. To pretend that we're always happy—or enthusiastic—would be inappropriate between spiritual friends. In fact, it can be truly harmful. We are all quite capable of deceiving ourselves about the most basic truths—for instance, that we're "moving ahead" quite well when, in fact, we're ignoring the truth; that is to say, we're putting ourselves back to sleep.

It is entirely possible for the spiritual path to take us through long periods of inner stagnation, loneliness, and even depression. Actually, I would expect this to happen. The experience must be understood on its own terms; and significant adjustments must be made in the way we live. All this is part of the spiritual path, rather than a departure from it. By coming to terms with these difficult times, we're able to move ahead on a more secure footing. To ignore it, on the other hand, can be a significant mistake, which I do not want you to make. You might, simply because of the sincerity of your enthusiasm! Believe me, it can happen to anyone, and I'm quite aware that my affirmation of you, although it's meant to be encouraging, could contribute to the same problem.

Let me suggest how you might avoid this trap: always be thankful for everything God has given you. Everyone knows this truth about thankfulness, but it's easier said than done. Why? Because we know there is "more," and we want it. We know there's more to the spiritual path, and we should want it. We know there's more love, and we want that too. The soul wants more; the ego wants more; and in wanting we forget what we already have.

The key is to remember that this "something more" is always found within the basics. What we want is never separate from the basics, and it will not be found somewhere else. I want you to think deeply about this. Do you remember the sacred gift you found only a short time ago? I'm talking about the love of your family and friends, and the love of God. Do you remember where you found it—in the wilderness? You probably can, but the memory fades with time. It's the wilderness of our lives that's easy to deny or forget, but this is also where we come to our senses. It's where our awakening begins and where God finds us. Memories of the wilderness are difficult and powerful. We push them away, after the fact, because we would rather forget. We want to "move ahead," as we should and must, but we must never, under any circumstances, leave the basics behind. That is always the danger in wanting to "move ahead."

I want the both of us to recall every possible detail about the wilderness, and compare it with the way we feel about ourselves now. This will help us appreciate how far we've come and how far we have to go. Even more, it will help us appreciate exactly *who* has been carrying us through the confusing times, the hard times, and the dark times. It will help us take responsibility for ourselves from a more realistic point of view—simply because we will perceive the ordinary illusions we wrap around ourselves more clearly. It will help us remember basic thankfulness, and this, more than anything else, will help us stay awake.

Let me sketch the broad picture I see unfolding in your life. Please don't take this as a personal criticism. I've been through exactly the same situation myself. Not very long ago, you became aware of something missing in your life. You felt a great deal of inner confusion and turmoil. You weren't a bad or immoral person. In fact, everything seemed to be going quite well. How strange it is that, outwardly, our lives seem to be thriving by any material standard, while, inwardly, the soul is starved for life. How could we have been so unaware? Where had we been? Even now, when life is better, some part of us remembers what it means to be spiritually lost. We remember even when the ego lures us to sleep again, which it would like to do. The ego refuses to admit that it might have been *that* mistaken, *that* wrong, *that* totally confused.

The turmoil passed in your life, as it did in mine. You were raised up, and now you've reach a plateau of sorts. You feel confident again and self-assured. I've encouraged you along these lines, telling you to trust your instincts, your gut feelings, and your common sense—which you have done. Life seems steady and secure again, and now you believe the time has come to move ahead. This, in itself, is good, but the problem lies in your gradual misperception of the real situation. In truth, the footing on this plateau is exceedingly slippery, and the balance you need is both difficult to find and easy to lose. You forget the basics. You're thankful, but for the wrong reasons—for example, you've gradually convinced yourself that you were the one who found God, when in fact it's God who always finds us. Once we deceive ourselves about this, then we are very close to losing our balance in everything else. Old habits return. We think we've figured out the spiritual path, when, in fact, we're becoming more confused with every passing day. The basic, fundamental truths lose their appeal and our minds are filled with enthusiasm for "something more."

By this shadowy kind of self-deception, the plateau transforms into another kind of place. Worldly successes become heavenly rewards, which should not be surprising—the ego adores anything remotely resembling outward proof of God's favor. Do you recognize this place? The ego announces its location every day: "I have been blessed by all that I've been given. The reason must be my faith." These are seemingly thankful words, but they're spoken with a presumptuous, complacent, and entirely self-congratulatory voice.

I hope you can recognize this within yourself. If you can, then you'll be in a much better position to stay awake. Do not believe that you're immune to such inner treachery. To claim the fruits of our actions, even in the name of God, is pure self-indulgence on the spiritual path, and it can become a world and a religion unto itself. This is the plateau that you have reached, and I could not agree more that it's time to move on. I know how pleasing the scenery can be, but I'm telling you that it's all a mirage. Open your eyes, and look again. Splash some cold water on your face. Do whatever is necessary to stay awake. Think about your family and friends. Have you convinced them of the same mirage? Perhaps your neighbors—all good people—suffer from the loss of work and illness. Does this mean they have slipped up, sinned, or lost the favor of God? Good things happen on the spiritual path, as well as bad. None of it is "deserved." And if the stock market takes a turn for the worse, or you lose your job, will you then lose your faith? I'll say it again: never believe you're immune to self-deception. I'm talking about pride. Pride is the purest form of treachery and it's easily mistaken for faith.

The whole point of my letter is to direct your attention to the basic, bedrock principle of the spiritual path. I'm thinking of the First Great Commandment: "I am the Lord, your God....you shall have no other Gods before me" (Exodus 20:2). As a belief, we all know it, but living this belief as a matter of faith is considerably more difficult. God always comes first. Not me, not you—but God. After a great deal of trial, error, and forgiveness, the spiritual path helps us realize that the love of God is our basic means of survival *and* the richest diet of solid, spiritual food we will ever have. Without it, the soul withers, no matter how far we believe we've come or how far we want to go. You would think this would be the very last thing we would forget or leave behind, but it happens, even in our enthusiasm and sometimes because of it.

I want you to reflect on what "something more" means to you. I'm suggesting that there is no hidden, secret teaching about faith that must be found and deciphered. I know how easy it is to believe there is. We believe that what we want must be found somewhere else. But if you want a formula, a principle, or a code to remember, then keep this in mind: first, the Spirit *descends*, calling us out of the darkness; and then, we are lifted up to follow the spiritual path. The order is important. We do *not* lift ourselves up, and then find God. To confuse the two is to put us in the driver's seat, rather than God, which means we've fallen back to sleep. God—the beginning, the end, and all points in between—is the reason we are able to take even one step.

If you can remember this with thankfulness and enthusiasm for all that you have received, then you'll be moving ahead on the spiritual path quite well. Otherwise, you'll be stuck, admiring a mirage of your own making. My counsel is to let go of thinking about your "progress," and to look for what is decent and right in your life every day. Unless you share your loving-kindness with others, especially with people who have less or nothing at all, then you will surely claim this plateau for yourself, making it the same shadowy world from which you were lifted only a short time ago. You may find yourself wondering, grim-faced, where Jesus has gone—"Why is he not here with me?" or "Why am I not there with him?"—as if you're the one who has been misunderstood, abandoned, and betrayed. The Bible teaches that Jesus always followed the spiritual path, carrying nothing but the basics.

Faithfully yours.

24. SIMPLICITY

My Dear Friend,

Today was an exceptionally good day. I ran some errands, made several phone calls, prepared for Sunday, visited a friend in the hospital, who is doing well, and then I went to town to talk with someone about an energy-efficient heating system for the church. Nothing eventful happened, nothing earthshaking, nothing newsworthy. But that's not the reason I call today a "good day." Usually, I'm struck by our resistance to having a good day when the opportunity presents itself. We seem to create reasons *not* to have a good day. You wouldn't think we would do this, but we do. Today, however, was different. It was not only a good day, it was exceptionally good; and I received it like a gift from on high. A cup of tea, ordinary conversation, some healthy laughter about ourselves—these are small miracles in a confused and confusing world. They help us awaken to the very real possibility that most days, in fact, can be exceptionally good.

There's no point in beating around the bush. I'm telling you all this because it speaks to the "simple life" you want and believe I have. God knows how long I've struggled with the simple life I believe I want. The ideal of "simplicity" is important on the spiritual path, and the fact that it's been such a struggle for me should tell you how supposedly "easy" it's been. Perhaps you should set aside some of those magazines devoted to "the simple life." I'm not saying that they're wrong. I just think it's time to get on with it.

Let me offer a few suggestions. First, make the decision to receive each day as it comes. Like most important things, this is easier said than done. You'll quickly realize that I'm asking you to enter the center of the cyclone, which means that you're on the right track. Develop a feel for your own inner struggle: the frustration, the resistance, the psychological games we habitually play each and every day. If you can do this, then you're more than halfway home. If you can find it within yourself to laugh about it, then you're even closer. Soon, you'll find the peace at the center, and that's what I really mean by an exceptionally good day. The key is to find it in the midst of your life as it normally happens. Do this, my friend, and you'll be following the spiritual path more faithfully than you ever have.

Strange as it may sound, our resistance to having an exceptionally good day lies within otherwise ordinary and healthy desires—for instance, the desire to be helpful. For the most part, we all want to be helpful people. It's good, moral, and deeply spiritual to want this. We want to be there when help is needed. We want to provide assistance and comfort when bad things happen. There's nothing wrong with this in any way. Yet this same desire can have an unexpected consequence. By a twisted kind of inner logic, we may feel good about ourselves when others feel bad. Unless a problem or emergency exists that requires our immediate attention, we don't quite know what to do. We lose our sense of purpose. To avert this inner "catastrophe," we might exaggerate some minor problems or create some new ones, just to feel useful and "good" about ourselves. It's weird, but it happens all the time. We work very hard to make the world a better place with our right hand, while making a mess of it with our left. That's how we become trapped in our own lives, which makes an exceptionally good day very difficult to find.

Second, it's important to recognize the difference between the life we have and the way we live it. The trap we set for ourselves is found somewhere in the middle, and spiritual traditions uphold the ideal of "simplicity" to help us avoid it. The problem comes with the way we apply this ideal. It helps to remember that life is not supposed to be simple. *Simplicity is not about life and the world. Simplicity is about how we live the lives we have been given.* It's totally absurd to wage an inner war against the world because it's not "simple" enough, when we can't manage to have even one good day when the opportunity arises. The human heart is complex by its very nature, just as God's creation is intricate, complicated, and magnificently diverse. Complexity, like diversity, is good. These are not problems that need to be solved or conditions in need of a cure. To believe we can make the world less complex in order to make our lives more simple is to create a great deal of unnecessary trouble—or worse. That's not a simpler life, but a nightmare in the making.

Having made the vows of a secular Franciscan, I can say with some confidence that the pursuit of simplicity does not involve making the world less complicated, any more than Francis's vow of poverty made his life forever simple. Yet, the profound Mystery so evident in the life of Saint Francis circles effortlessly around one elusive ideal—simplicity. For me, this ideal symbolizes the spiritual path as a whole. The path may not be easy, but it is simple. God is not somewhere else, but here. We don't have to become someone else.

All we have to do is break free of our own selves. I've known people who have experienced the ecstasy of God's presence in moments of deep prayer and meditation, but have a terrible time living their lives every day. They're still as trapped within their own lives and selves as they were before. The little-known truth is that moments of mystical bliss are not difficult to find. With some patience, discipline, and devotion, anyone can experience them. But the spiritual path really begins when we find that same holy love within ourselves, and then live it within our lives every day.

Several years ago, I made a pilgrimage to Assisi, hoping to form my own impressions about who Saint Francis was. After a long bus ride, I arrived at the hotel completely exhausted. It was late in the day, so I found a nearby restaurant and then returned to my room to get some rest before visiting the basilica the following morning. I sat on the floor to do my prayers, which is my usual way. As it turned out, the remaining hours of the evening were anything but routine. While I prayed, the words that formed in my mind were straightforward and clear: "Every day counts. . . . Do not waste one moment. . . . Get on with it. . . . What are you waiting for?" A wall of sorts, which had been building in me over many years, finally collapsed, and I cried throughout the night. These were fiery tears. Hour after hour, they wouldn't stop. By morning, I realized that Francis had done something most of us would never think of doing. He must have taken responsibility for his life in the most radical way possible. He would have known that there was no one to blame for his discontent, so he just stopped laying blame. My guess is that he even stopped blaming himself. And when he did, he was filled with love. The end result was that he not only found God, he learned the secret of making every day exceptionally good.

The soul knows how trapped we are in our own lives. The spiritual path helps us become aware of this, sometimes unbearably, until the day arrives and we come face to face with the painful difference between what the heart knows—that God is real—and what our everyday lives seem to be like. I could have been anywhere—at home, in Assisi, in the remotest place at the end of the earth; but in that moment, the possibility of blaming anyone, even myself, had vanished into thin air. We are the only ones who can take responsibility for how we live, and we are the only ones who can prevent it. The choice is entirely ours to make. Think of the alternative: we can carry on as before, secretly waiting for a bad day to happen so we might feel good about ourselves!

My friend, of course you want a simpler life. We all do, and you're right to want it. My suggestion is to take what you believe seriously—that God is real—by taking responsibility for how *you* live every day. Imagine yourself in the shoes of Saint Francis. Don't put him on a pedestal. Imagine him as a person like you. Imagine yourself, like I did, walking about Assisi. It's a wonderful place, beautiful, picturesque, and far from the busy streets of Rome. It qualifies as a small town in my eyes, and in Francis's day, eight hundred years ago, it would have been smaller. The truth is that he felt so much discontent with life in Assisi that he fled, leaving behind everything he owned. His actions had virtually no relation to feelings of nostalgia or quaint images of "the simpler life" we might have today. The countryside is no simpler than the city, not really. Ask the farmers where I live or the families with school-age children, and they will tell you the same. The discontent in the heart of Saint Francis went far beyond nostalgic images of simplicity or anything we might read about in magazines. He created quite a scene when he left. People's feelings were hurt. The townsfolk in Assisi thought he was crazy—a lunatic, a fanatic. This one person whose life has inspired so many ordinary people to follow the Christian path was almost declared a heretic. Today, he would almost definitely be placed under government surveillance; but, in reality, he was only taking responsibility for his life.

I'm asking you to be practical. Saint Francis suffered awful illnesses and other troubles, yet he knew the meaning of a good day perhaps better than anyone ever has. He didn't dwell on evil in the world, although his time was probably as corrupt as ours. From the Spirit's point of view, there was nothing extreme about the meaning of his actions or his resolve. All he really did was to claim the goodness of God as the center of his life. He also made the rather obvious point that our possessions take possession of us. By the sheer energy we give them, they define who we are, how we feel, and what our aspirations will be: *I have, therefore I am. I can decide what to buy, therefore I must be free.* Can you feel the weight of it, the triumphant logic that rules the soul and distorts what goodness really is? Would you call that a truly good day? I don't think so, but we act as if it is. This makes us the fanatics, the lunatic majority, who would like the whole world to pursue this same shadowy image of goodness—and simplicity.

It's much easier to dismiss simplicity, to explain away Francis, and to rationalize our lives as they are, than it is to have a really good day. We tell ourselves that he was not like us, that he was "special," which is our way of holding him accountable to our egos—in effect, blaming him for our shortcomings. After all, we have families to feed, children to raise, bills to pay, and checkbooks to balance. This is true enough, but it's not entirely true. The light that illumined the heart of Saint Francis is the same light that breaks through within us when we say "enough is enough" about spending money and having more things. It's easy to say "enough is enough" about others, but have we ever really said it about ourselves? Have we heard our own hearts say, "Get on with it, stop wasting your life with this nonsense"—and then actually chosen to live in a simpler way? I'm not saying that I've got this all sorted out in my life, but I am telling you that the Spirit really does speak to us in this way. I'm asking you to take the time to listen.

The pursuit of a simpler life is not a way to close our eyes to the world's problems. Perhaps the best place to begin is by learning to care for what we have and to give away what we don't need. It is simply not true that happiness depends on having more, and I can guarantee you that our goodness does not depend on bad things happening to other people. It's a rather obvious fact that we've become trapped in our own lives, and it may take a while to work our way out. But by following the spiritual path, one day at a time, the possessions we have will possess us less, the ones we want will matter less, and the people, God's living beings, and life itself—these will mean a great deal more. If all goes well, we might learn what it means to have a really good day. And maybe, if all goes exceptionally well, we might share that day with others, not because we believe they need it, but because we simply like to be in their company.

Faithfully yours.

25. NEEDING AND WANTING

My Dear Friend,

Our conversation on the phone yesterday happened none too soon. I realize how difficult that call must have been to make, and I'm glad you did. I admire your courage as much as your honesty. Financial debt affects everything, as you know all too well. It can exact an emotional toll so great that the result is unbearable despair. You could not have said it better: "Enough is enough."

This, my friend, will be a huge turning point on the spiritual path. Its significance may someday surpass the time, nearly a year ago, when we first became friends. Then, you were struggling with "the God question," and dealing with some shattered illusions about yourself and the world. Now, the time has come to pick up all the pieces that remain. I'm aware that moods can swing unpredictably in times of crisis, and I may be taking an unnecessary risk by continuing the direct, straightforward tone of our conversation. Nonetheless, my greater concern is that you might become disillusioned and cynical because of this situation, and make decisions you would regret in the better times that will surely come. I trust your judgment, which is sound regardless of your low opinion of yourself at this moment. I only want you to use your judgment well by accepting the support of your friends. Keep your wits about you, and avoid any impulsive or otherwise hasty decisions. This is a difficult time, but in the long run, it can be more liberating than you realize now. You have good instincts. You know what to do. Having said that, the purpose of my letter is to offer encouragement along the lines we previously discussed—simplifying your life in every respect.

I'm sorry the debt has cast such a dark shadow for so long, yet I am pleased that you have faced it with the humility and grace that God has given you in great abundance. "Enough is enough"—these are powerful words when applied to ourselves with wisdom and resolve. I heard clarity of intent when you spoke them on the phone, but I detected anger too. Of course you feel angry, and I'm confident that you will understand what it means and not be overcome by it. In the days ahead, just remember that the way we act upon our emotions matters a very great deal.

But there was more in your voice—call it "acceptance." I found that to be very hopeful, and even reassuring. Sometimes the world serves up a severe blow. We think this could not happen, not to me; but it can, and it has. Whenever we take a long, honest look at our problems and examine how we have contributed to them, instead of blaming others, then the soul has the opportunity to grow. Obviously, another "growth experience" is not what you want at this time in your life, but here it is. Your response to the whole situation will have the power to transform those shattered illusions into something of immense good. In this way, the world, as brutal and unforgiving as it can sometimes be, is not our enemy. The world is a witness to our lives. Even more, the world participates in our awakening. The world is changed by what we do, just as we are changed by everything that happens.

I know you want your life back, and you know that the debt must be eliminated as soon as possible. Decisions must be made, without delay, about those dangerous credit cards. My letter is meant to be encouraging in every respect, and I want you to understand that these practical measures are only the beginning of the responsibility you sincerely want to take. They may keep you out of the red in the future, but you must also thoroughly examine the causes of the debt down to its deepest root. Although this will not be easy, you can do it and it must be done.

Despite some truly irresponsible behavior with your bank account, you have always been a responsible person, which adds to the confusion about how this situation was created in the first place. It's no wonder that you're asking, "How could this have happened to me?" This is what you want to know, and it is a very good question. I want you to understand that taking more responsibility will not, in itself, address the heart of the issue before you now. The issue at stake here is "redemption." I use this word carefully. Redemption begins, inwardly, with a change of heart. I heard you take the first step when you said, "Enough is enough." Redemption does not consist in telling ourselves, repeatedly, how bad, sinful, or irresponsible we have been. Wallowing in the mire will not help you or anyone else. Instead, use your resolve—and the anger—to avoid making the same mistakes again. You may not believe you can do this, but you can. God has faith in you, so have some confidence in yourself, and let the two of you—God and you—transform how you live, outwardly. Tradition says that Christ's death on the cross was God's way of demonstrating that the darkness in our souls can be overcome. The purpose of his ultimate sacrifice was not God's way of helping us to pay our bills, so we can buy more, more responsibly, guilt-free to the end of our days.

If you really want your freedom, then you must also want to simplify your life. Think of it as a new pattern or structure for living, and make it your spiritual practice. I realize that we usually consider "structure" to be punishment, but nothing could be further from the truth. Be creative and flexible, while pursuing it with every ounce of no-nonsense determination you have—like your life depends on it. Structure is good. It gives the soul a place to call "home," a place to relax and breathe more freely.

Let's face it: the structure you have now depletes the soul, as well as your bank account. It's based, at least in part, on making trips to the mall. I'm serious about this. How often do we say to ourselves that happiness will be found when we own this one more special thing? It seems so reasonable at the time. So we buy it, and the same impulse returns the following day or the next, just as it was before. This is the way the world operates, and I wonder whether it represents the life you want back—perpetually wanting more, while having so much more than we need, when so many people have nothing. Is that really what you want? I'm not saying that money and beautiful things are wrong or evil. Yet the desire to have more stuff feels like an insatiable beast feeding on the soul, much like the dread of those monthly bills breathing down your neck. Who are we kidding? Debt or no debt, we must come to terms with the difference between "needing" and "wanting." We already know that being a responsible person cannot possibly mean that every want and desire "should" be fulfilled or that material wants will meet our spiritual needs.

I realize you feel isolated, confused, and ashamed. Trust me. You are not alone in this. I can tell you, as a friend and as a priest, that I know a large number of responsible but miserable people who find themselves in exactly the same situation. You were right on the telephone—we have lost our reason, which becomes all the more apparent when the bills arrive, as they always do. We are all in the mire, and this dreadful situation screams out for redemption.

In no way am I asking you to be accountable to me personally, but we are all accountable—to God and each other. My advice is to remember two of the promises we make at baptism: *to resist evil* and *to respect the dignity of every human being*. These promises can be the foundation of your new pattern for living, and—if I may—let me suggest how you might put them into practice. In the morning, before the busyness of the day takes hold of your life, sit quietly for a few minutes and make this commitment:

Regardless of anything else that may happen, good or bad, I will do my best, on this day, to live within my means, to take care of myself and my family, and to help someone in need.

It really can be that simple. Don't spend money you don't have. Make an inventory of what you really need—the list will be surprisingly small. Actually listen to what people say—this will help you remember the difference between needing and wanting. Take some spare food and clothing to a shelter. Eat in a healthy way. Do everything possible to reduce how much you poison your body, the land, the water, and the air. Pollution is a form of debt too, which affects every form of life. Like irresponsible children, we've been depending on Mother Nature to absorb our bad spending habits much too long, and there comes a point when she can no longer carry us along. You can do all this, my friend. Many lives will improve, including yours, and you will be a happier person for sure. The truth is that we all must do this. It's a matter of survival.

Faithfully yours.

26. RESISTING EVIL

My Dear Friend,

Thank you so much for the news of your family. I'm always pleased to hear about any part of your life; whether it's the kids at school, your work, your lives at home, or your reflections on the spiritual path—it's all good. I'm also intrigued by some comments you make near the end of your letter, where you speculate about the state of the world and then say, "Maybe evil is more than a fantasy or myth. . . . It could be real." I believe that you're asking a question, but I can't be sure. And you've given no clear indication of why you've brought this up, or what you mean by "evil." I assume that you're referring to evil spirits, the devil, Satan, and so on. My first reaction is to wonder what you really have in mind—it could be anything. Perhaps one of your children was disturbed by the "late night, fright night" movies. Or is this your response to hearing speeches about geopolitics and terrorism? Perhaps the brief mention of it in my last letter piqued your curiosity, and now you want to pin me down.

If you are asking a question, then this one is more complicated than you might believe. The question itself is great, but the implication of asking it concerns me a great deal. I'm thinking of Pandora's Box. You haven't done anything wrong. I'm not suggesting that you've unleashed forces that you'll later regret. Pandora's Box is already open. You can tell it is by the way the word "evil" rolls off the lips of people so easily these days. It gives the impression that we, as a people, feel more certain about the existence of evil in the world—in the world out there—than about the meaning of our faith. That makes me feel uneasy, and I want to discourage you from going anywhere near it. Like I said, I'm not really sure what you have in mind, and I don't know what kind of answer you're looking for, but my advice is to keep your mind focused on resisting evil in your life every day, rather than the possibility of evil as an "entity" in the world.

My answer to your question is that evil is definitely real. Yet the problem with definitive statements like that is that they can be true *and* misleading at the same time. Let me explain. You, for example, may be utterly convinced that evil is real, but unless you're aware of how evil works within yourself, then your belief is virtually useless. I want you to understand that the answer I gave is only words. Words are good; words can be powerful, but evil knows how to hide behind them. It can hide just as easily behind "Evil is real" as behind "Evil is an illusion." My answer seems to be direct and to the point, but it only seems that way. In reality, it doesn't explain or clarify anything. It only begs the question of what you consider reality to be like, and that involves *you*. Your awareness is not separate from the question you have asked, and your answer (as well as mine) depends on your capacity and willingness to discern the difference between reality and fantasy in your own life. Do you think that's easy? Where evil is concerned, I don't believe it is.

You need to realize that evil works through the power of deception—which, one might argue, is entirely dependent on our willingness to be deceived. Evil tells us that we're doing the right thing, when it's wrong; and that we're doing the wrong thing, when it's right. It leads us to believe that we have no power to do the right thing, when we do; and all the power in the world, when the only real power is God's. It tries to convince us that the world, other people, or anything we want is simply ours for the taking. Evil tells us that it's not only good to have it, but that we should have it—that it's rightly ours and it's God's will. It's a simple argument really, surprisingly convincing, especially when the pressure is on, and always clever. Why? Because it's the same old story, repeated again and again, and evil knows that the ego will listen.

Ultimately, the whole argument fails for one simple reason: the only true spiritual reality is God's love, and nothing can overcome it. That's why I'm saying that the only real question about evil that really matters involves you. Can *you* perceive that the line separating reality from fantasy is not so clearly drawn? That evil is a master of hiding behind the appearance of respectability, goodness, and common sense? Evil is real, but have you understood that the more important question is whether God is real? *Evil wants you to believe in the reality of evil.* We all know how it works. We know it in our hearts and in our minds. Despite that, in the moment when deception comes, we're quite likely to believe something else. This is what evil wants to know about us: Do we know that God is real? Do we believe in the power of God's love?

It is absolutely necessary to resist evil in your life every day. But ultimately the only place that you or anyone else can resist the power of evil and win is within yourself—with the help of God. The best way to resist evil is to avoid becoming preoccupied by it in your thoughts. That's what I mean by Pandora's Box. It's already open—the forces of chaos, confusion, and deception have already been released—but that doesn't mean you have to stick your head in. On the one hand, you should never, ever, go out looking for evil. On the other hand, you must resist believing that other people or groups of people are more prone to evil thoughts and deeds than you are. Be vigilant, without becoming preoccupied by it. Evil feeds on fascination and fear, so the less attention you give to it, the better. Instead, keep your heart and mind focused on the goodness you see every day and the love of God. Your thoughts will remain much more wholesome that way, and you will have done a respectable job in putting up a spirited resistance.

Concerning Jesus, tradition says quite clearly that he healed and exorcised many people of "unclean spirits." Concerning us, I would suggest that we're probably much more familiar with "unclean spirits" than we usually realize. Simply reflect on the seemingly smaller evils in life, and take them seriously, rather than conjuring up sensationalized ones in your mind. I am thinking of pride, greed, lust, envy, gluttony, anger, sloth—the traditional seven deadly sins. These sins only seem to be ordinary, and it would be exceedingly unwise to see them as any less "deadly" than the demons that you and your children see on the screen. For example, you've recently told me that your children have been subjected to some bullying at school. I might see that as a form of evil—not the people, but the behavior—manifesting one or more of the "deadly sins." I'm also sorry to hear that bullying has become so commonplace these days, including "cyber-bullying," and you are right to take it seriously now. Otherwise, the consequences for them can go far beyond anything you have the power to control.

So how can you help your children resist being bullied? First, the issue must be addressed at its first appearance. Give it no opportunity to take root in their lives and thoughts. I would teach your children to resist by laughing. This will cleanse their hearts and minds of any lasting harmful impact. Second, your children must know that they've done nothing wrong. Third, it must be brought to the attention of the officials at school. I believe that you've done all these things already. If so, you've done a good job. You haven't ignored or overlooked the trauma your children must feel, and you've taken the appropriate actions. Often bullying is ignored or brushed aside, which only tells everyone that this kind of behavior can be tolerated—that it's acceptable—when, in fact, people don't want to deal with it. The result is that more and more children join in. They become willing or unwilling participants, learning to accept these destructive habits, carrying them into their lives as adults. In the meantime, a whole lot of people get hurt. This is how the great evils of our time begin.

I want to tell you about a similar incident I witnessed at school in my childhood. An "unclean spirit" was involved. If I were to give the spirit a name, I would call it "greed," although there was probably more than that involved. Think of greed as the desire to take whatever we want at any cost, which means that greed does not necessarily revolve around money. I hope this story will help you understand how real the potential for evil can be within us, and why resisting it precisely there is so important.

Bill and his family were newcomers in town. We were in the fourth grade, and I could plainly see the shyness in his face when he first came to school. He was having a difficult time with the adjustment, as anybody would. It's awfully hard for anyone to make new friends in a new place. A few weeks later, our teacher did something that made everyone nervous, including Bill. She gave us a special assignment. Each student had to recite the same short poem at the front of the whole class. You may know that Americans generally dislike speaking in public. Studies show that we fear this even more than nuclear war. So, being normal American kids, we were petrified by the assignment.

The inevitable day arrived, as we all feared. Following the alphabetized class roster, we each took our appointed turn. Everyone did quite well, or well enough, except for Bill. As he was standing behind the small, pint-sized podium, reciting the poem, we all noticed that he was acting in a peculiar way. Suddenly, he fell to the floor with a loud thump. The sound was startling. None of us had ever seen an epileptic seizure, or knew what one was, and we all were shocked and disturbed. The teacher handled it well. Calmly, she instructed us to sit quietly at our desks, while she took care of Bill. An eternity seemed to pass before he got up, but he finally did. He was bleeding slightly from his nose; but otherwise, he seemed to be okay. The teacher placed her arm around his shoulders and led him to the lounge. The principal was notified, and he called his parents.

During lunch, one of my fellow students, wanting to draw attention to himself, made fun of Bill. He spoke at great length about how peculiar Bill looked when he was lying on the floor. To make matters worse, he performed a cruel imitation of the seizure, which set off a current of unkind talk among some of the students. For a few moments, two or three more joined in, but others who witnessed this cruel incident felt uncomfortable with what they saw and turned away.

Everything I saw in the cafeteria that day was burned in my memory. But it was something about me that I really want you to understand. All that I have told you so far describes how an "unclean spirit"—the intent of the boy who was greedy for attention—works outwardly in the world we all inhabit. Our capacity to resist evil depends on our willingness to recognize how evil works, inwardly, and then to do something about it. The whole process begins when we become open to "ordinary" temptations, like greed or envy. For a few moments, we may feel a force, of sorts, within ourselves. It makes us feel frozen inside. Time seems to stand still. I'm not saying this is either "natural" or "supernatural," but it touches upon a vulnerable and tender part of the soul, where evil can take root—unless we resist.

As the mean-spirited incident at lunch was taking place, I wondered what a classmate of mine was thinking. She was the girl in class whom I fancied. I wondered whether she would go along with the ridicule, so I watched her closely. If she did participate, I thought to myself, then I might join in too. It would give me the opportunity to become her friend. Those were, in fact, my thoughts for a few frozen seconds. I will never forget it. Even more, I wondered what it would mean if I didn't play along with the ridicule: Would I become an object of ridicule myself, and then lose any hope of getting close to the girl of my dreams? All these seductive thoughts filled my mind while Bill was being ridiculed. That is how evil works. The boy who ridiculed Bill was greedy for attention, and his greed drew out the greed in me. I resisted, but the experience of it made a lasting impression. In that moment, I learned how subtle evil is, and how strong the temptation can be.

Jesus taught that the mere thought of sin was as bad as actually doing it. I don't know how you feel about that. On the surface, it seems rather stern and severe, but we all understand his meaning. In the fourth grade, I learned that he was right. Sometimes our inner thoughts show traces of genuine brutality—crude, icy, and calculating—and the world turns completely around "me" and what "I" might gain. This is the presence of "greed," the "unclean spirit," not as an abstract idea of sin, but the real thing living in our midst and within us. It makes us shudder to realize the evil we are capable of doing. If we go along once, then the next time will be easier, and then easier after that. As grim as this sounds, we all know the truth of it. Jesus was right. My experience helps me understand why the church in history has been so reluctant to minimize the depraved condition of the human heart. We don't like to hear it, but that is the very thing we're so prone to overlook or deny.

The spiritual path does not require us to believe any particular theology or theory about evil. Speculative insights based on experience might help us along the way, but ultimately, they are only speculations. Evil does exist—just open your eyes—as does our temptation to ignore it, while believing we are innocent. Yet the smaller evils are the ones that concern me the most. They have a habit of taking root. The spiritual path cannot be followed until we learn to resist this potential for evil within ourselves. Everyone is involved; and in some respect, all our hands are bloody.

One last comment about the story: in my view, an "unclean spirit" tried to find a home in my school, and I'm glad to say it was unsuccessful. A few days after this happened, my mother suggested that I go home with Bill to play and have dinner, which I did. We became friends. In the lives we live every day, rather than in the movies, that's what the resistance of evil and the healing of "unclean spirits" really look like.

Faithfully yours.

27. COMMUNION AND CREATION

My Dear Friend,

Once, I made a promise to you, almost in passing, about fly-fishing. You were interested then, and I wonder if you still are. Just say the word and I'll be ready to go, rain or shine. My close-to-home friends would definitely smile about this, and I suspect your thoughts are much like theirs. For me, fly-fishing is not only "like" religion, it can actually be a form of prayer; and if the truth be told, I have known times of full-blown communion on a trout stream. That, of course, is why I risk making a caricature of myself and my vocation, but I don't really care anymore. I've lost count of the rivers that have baptized me, and I have learned to smile when I see those compassionate, forgiving looks in the eyes of my friends. They've probably read Norman MacLean's magnificent book, *A River Runs Through It,* or seen the movie, which is beautiful too. There's the part about Saint Peter being a fisherman and Jesus telling his disciples he would make them "fishers of men"—now, of course, we say "fishers of people," which is much better. I like inclusive language very much and use it, but as a priest who fishes for people and fish, I know we aren't going to get the words right all the time. I also know that too many words spoken along the river will make me head upstream. My point: the best lessons in life are learned in the stillness before words are spoken or a line is cast. That sums up pretty well the purpose of my letter. I want you to know how I learned about the stillness, and how my love for fishing has been the thread that weaves it all together. As you read what I have to say, you'll understand that it's not really about fishing. It's about following our hearts and letting God find us.

I should tell you now that learning how to be still is the first truly essential lesson in fly-fishing. Outward stillness is good, but inner stillness is better. As it often happens, I learned this first from my father. He was walking ahead, crouching carefully under the branches of a large stand of rhododendron. We were making our way to a small stream only a few yards away. Each step I took matched his. I remember noticing how big he seemed and how easy it was for me, tiny tot that I was, to walk through the thicket. Contrary to otherwise well-deserved stereotypes, adults often have a more difficult time being still than children. I've seen dogs and cats who are completely nonplussed by noisy kids, but an adult who harbors aggressive feelings will make them—pets and kids—run away and hide.

We learn most everything by the example of adults, perhaps the greater part being the emotions that shape our world. My father taught me about stillness way back then, and I'm glad he did. Almost by definition, "growing up" means losing the inner stillness that is naturally ours, which creates a big problem for our spiritual lives and for fly-fishing. Trout scatter faster than the wind if we enter their world as a rowdy intruder. Like the sages of old, they're attuned to subtle changes in sound and qualities of light. If they don't see you coming or your shadow stretching across the water, they can feel your vibration through soil and rocks.

The beauty of it is that we are all capable of stillness. Even when we bring our inner disturbances to the river, along with too much fishing gear, all is not lost. The sound of flowing water quiets the mind like a mantra. Let yourself be still enough to hear it, and the Spirit will respond, teaching us what we really need to know. I received my first lesson in the sacred art of prayer that afternoon with my father, without realizing it. That is how my love for fly-fishing began.

I never told anyone about this next part. It's no big deal, I suppose, but at the time, it was one of those sacred things we tend to keep to ourselves. In any event, I'll tell you now. Fishing was my salvation in high school. After work in the summers and sometimes at the end of the school day, I visited a nearby lake where my family kept a small boat. One year I refused to participate in springtime sports, despite my love for them, only because I wanted to be near the water. My sole aim was to cast that fishing rod and get as far from the drama of teenage social life as I possibly could. Life on the phone was suffocating, and I'm sure most of my friends felt the same way. It can magnify our insecurities and fears to the point of depression, which leads to self-medication as a way of life for far too many people. All teenagers struggle with this or adapt to it the best they can. My way was to go fishing. The stillness gave me sanctuary and refuge in the true spiritual sense. The placid water of the lake cleansed my soul, maybe not as much as a mountain stream, but it worked. I sorted out my strained emotions in the late afternoons, until the brilliant red covered the water and me at sunset. I loved those moments. Call it "fishing" if you like, but with the water and the sun as my witnesses, I call it "prayer."

I made a fateful decision while fishing on that lake. I wanted to live a life without the need for sanctuary, and I was determined to find it. I had no desire whatsoever to conform to the drama and carry it with me forevermore. It didn't seem real, and I wanted the freedom to be myself. Looking back now, it seems ironic that I didn't take a fishing rod with me to college. Yet it was probably a good decision. I was so determined to make a new start that if I had taken it, I doubt it would have been used. My fishing rod was replaced by books and study.

On the other hand, I didn't leave everything behind. Most of my time reading was spent by a small pond only a short walk from the campus. The stillness of the water was teaching me even then. The more I read—William Blake, Walker Percy, and Margaret Mead come to mind now—the more I wanted to know how people in different parts of the world live and how they experience God. I decided that I was going to do exactly that, and I did. It was a good decision. I can't remember ever sitting down and praying about this, but it was a prayerful decision too. I loved being alive with every step I took, and I found what I was looking for. What I discovered is that our experiences of God may be very different, but people everywhere recognize the difference between crass manipulation and true holiness. We all know when life is tragic and funny. It doesn't matter how different our languages, religions, and cultures might be. We can see the truth about life in each other's eyes.

While all this was taking place, I never really left behind my need for sanctuary. In fact, I actually made it my spiritual path. I was looking for refuge in a world that seemed confused and out of control. But gradually I realized that the more I followed this path, the more the ground seemed to fall away under my feet. I want you to think carefully about what I'm telling you because it would be easy to misinterpret. The problem was not the path itself. I was searching for the presence of God everywhere, and I was finding it. This not only deepened my feel for the sacredness of life, but also opened my eyes to a magnitude of human suffering that statistics or the media cannot possibly portray. I witnessed the whole earth becoming horribly impoverished—the people and the planet—and my search for sanctuary revealed how little sanctuary there is left to find, for anyone, anywhere. The world is undergoing a crisis of the Spirit on a massive scale. No one wants this to happen, but it is.

The meaning of this finally hit home one afternoon, when I was visiting my mom and dad at their home in the Blue Ridge Mountains. Family gatherings are good opportunities to reminisce, and I wanted to be with them and to relive the stillness I had known in my youth. With fishing rod in hand, I headed toward the pond and a small boat behind their new house. Within a few minutes, I felt a fish tug the end of my line. When I finally reeled it in, I was startled by the large number of cysts covering the entire body of the fish. For reasons I didn't understand in that moment, I felt so shaken and unsteady that I had to go ashore. I'm not a squeamish person, and the sight of diseased creatures—including people—was nothing new to me, so my reaction was entirely unexpected. I waited a few minutes, and then, realizing that something more was going on, I went indoors, lay on the sofa, and hovered in a dreamlike state for nearly an hour.

Something was emerging from a deep place in my soul—a new awareness, a truth about myself that I had hidden. I didn't know what it was, but it was happening of its own accord, and I couldn't stop it. My mother was sitting across the room. I saw her watching with some concern, but trusting, at the same time, in my judgment. I prayed, trying to find the stillness I had known before, and within a few moments, the answer I sought was looking back at me. It was an image of my hands holding the diseased fish. In the purely literal sense, I may have caught him on the end of my line; but spiritually, the fish had caught me. Countless thoughts raced through my mind. I remembered the fish as a symbol of the sacred in Christianity and many other traditions. I wondered what Jesus would have said if the disciples had been catching diseased fish in the Sea of Galilee. I wondered what the miracle of loaves and fishes would have meant. Poisoned fish = poisoned water = poisoned people. It is that simple. Jesus, I told myself, might have healed the fish and the people, and done even more about the sea.

I remembered those moments of sanctuary by the lake in high school and all the conflict and self-doubt that went with those tumultuous years. That's the time in our lives when we first learn what "growing up" means. For many, this involves medicating our confused hearts, pushing the soul out of the body, and flirting dangerously with death. There on the sofa, I began to put it all together: if communion with God is what we want, then we must learn to live again in our bodies. Our bodies are God's creation in human form, and our senses are glorious gifts to help us experience the presence of God. I understood that the spiritual path is about life. Communion with God, holy sanctuary, the spiritual path—these can never be an escape from the problems of this world, and especially from the web of life. For years, I had been searching and escaping at the same time. This had never been my purpose or intent, but it was the truth. It was the reason I felt the ground falling away under my feet; and now, reality was staring me in the face in the form of a small, sick, and suffering fish.

Nearly twenty years later, I've taken up fly-fishing again—rather seriously. I love it more than I can possibly say. It's my sanctuary, my refuge, and a time of prayerful communion. I can always find the stillness when I'm fly-fishing. Earlier I said that the first essential lesson in fishing is learning to be still. This is true, but I have learned the second lesson that follows from the first. Ultimately, God is our sanctuary, and the best way to find it is to care for what we have been given as an act of faith and thanksgiving. We do not have the right to do anything we please, especially when it puts life at risk. The web of life sustains all life. Without it, there would be no jobs, no families, no churches, synagogues, or mosques. No sacred space of any kind. Nothing that anyone anywhere holds dear. There would be no spiritual path. We would not exist.

I'm telling you that it's not enough to want sanctuary, refuge, even communion with God for ourselves. If fly-fishing gives me sanctuary, then I must learn the ways of the rivers, the insects, the kingfishers, muskrats, and bears—and help to give them sanctuary too. And when I go home, I must help those who have lost touch with the stillness to find it within themselves. Caring about this is terribly important, but caring is not enough. Caring becomes benign neglect when we fail to put it into practice, and there's no such thing as "benign neglect." We're all in this together, my friend, and together is the way we will learn to live again.

Faithfully yours.

28. LOVING-KINDNESS

My Dear Friend,

Not long ago—maybe it's been a few months—I wrote to you about the difference between "being right" and "being loving." At the time, I made this distinction simply because I wanted you to reflect on it. But now, after some time has passed, I want to raise it again: Which is the more reliable way to follow the spiritual path? I realize that answers to questions like this are not always clear-cut, but I'll repeat again what I said before: my answer is "by being kind." Loving-kindness is everything. And I'll tell you again why this is important. Often, we feel so "right" in the conviction of our beliefs that we're willing to defend them to the bitter end, while showing little, if any, love. It can take a long time to appreciate the implications of this within ourselves. A significant change in heart is required, and the most profound realization—namely, that the spiritual path revolves much less around "my faith," "my religion," and "my beliefs" than we usually think. Given the entrenched emphasis on "me" in modern times, any change of heart along these lines amounts to a spiritual passage in its own right—and it can be very difficult. The purpose of my letter is to help you understand what this passage means, and hopefully, to help you make the leap.

I want to be as honest and straightforward as I can about this. Before telling you a personal story, let me spell out some basic principles. As a rule, we want "the truth, the whole truth, and nothing but the truth" in matters of religion and faith. We want to have confidence to know that our faith is true and reliable, and that our beliefs place us on solid ground, spiritually—which is entirely right and understandable. As Christians, for example, we take refuge in Jesus' teaching: "I am the way, and the truth, and the life" (John 14:6, NRSV). Yet our minds deceive us if we fail to recognize that the spiritual path must be followed for its truth to be realized. This means that the best way—perhaps the only way—to "defend" any sacred truth is by living that truth in our own lives; that is to say, by following the spiritual path. No one else can do this for us. Unless this path is actually followed, then religion becomes a set of ideas, an intellectual game, and probably a grab for power.

The problem comes with the personal nature of faith. The fact that faith is personal makes it all the more powerful. Even in the best of times, our desire to know the truth, to have the truth for our own, and to defend it, wraps tightly around our identity as individuals—around our sense of "me" and "mine." So, instead of truly defending our beliefs by following the path, we become defensive about them, which makes it very difficult to hear different points of view or to understand the lived experience of people unlike ourselves. Nevertheless, truths about God and life are always known through the experience of actual people. Take the Bible as a case in point. The Bible is a collection of the experiences of a large number of people—spoken, remembered, handed down in poetry and song, written down, and translated in many different languages and forms. All experience, including faith, involves different perspectives. In a very real sense, the Bible is a collection of perspectives—not one, but many.

We can't wish this away, and we shouldn't want to. Human life, by its very nature, is based on multiple points of view. This is the way things are, and it should be the last thing we would resist, but we often do. In fact, strong institutional pressures work to keep our resistance in place. We can feel those pressures whenever our beliefs begin to change as we live and grow. A few hundred years ago, millions of people, not only churchgoers, discovered that they were wrong in their belief that all the heavens revolve around the earth. This did not mean that God loved them or us any less. In the same way, new scientific or historical evidence that challenges the content of any belief does not have to threaten a person's identity as a Christian. Jesus' teaching—"I am the way, and the truth, and the life"—is still true. At its heart, this "way" is a path of love, rather than a defense of being right.

Perhaps our resistance to following the path of love involves the habit of regarding our glimpses of sacred truths— which are partial and limited by their very nature—as the whole truth. Let's say that you have a personal experience of God—a relationship with Jesus—and that you're a sincerely devout person. Does this mean that you know the whole truth about God and faith? Is your experience something more than one person's perspective? We might claim that it is—which is the very point you have been wrestling with. This is a very healthy and honest struggle, and I'm glad it is happening. But I want to ask you this: Is your struggle really about God, or are we really talking about your personal identity? Faith is personal, but faith fused and confused with personal identity is an altogether different matter.

Let me give another kind of example. My experience is that a single breath of air tells me, with authority, that the atmosphere really does exist. I love breathing, I love the atmosphere. The atmosphere keeps me alive. Yet that single breath is not an experience of the whole atmosphere. It is the same with the experience of God. God can be known personally. God can be known as a person. This is entirely true. But the experience itself is not the whole story. Every breath we will ever take will not reveal the whole truth about God. Does this mean we should stop breathing? Absolutely not. Should we be afraid of taking another breath because our beliefs might change? Absolutely not. The path of love is a way of taking each and every breath with our hearts and minds open to God's infinite presence. I believe Jesus wants us to take another breath, even when that means understanding who he is in a different way, and who we are, as people of faith, in a more faithful way.

Now, let's take one more step. There comes a point when we confront the sometimes brutal fact that faith, religion, and the spiritual path are really not about "me." We begin to understand that the spiritual path really is about God—and God is love. When this happens, questions and concerns about personal identity lose their strong grip on our faith. Different perspectives and experiences, different beliefs, religions, and whole ways of life are no longer the problem or threat that we once imagined them to be. In fact, they can provoke us to understand the Holy Mystery better and appreciate how beautiful those sacred truths really are. For that reason, I hope you will never surrender loving-kindness to the kind of defensive righteousness that I suspect you're considering. Keep listening to your heart and learn. Let the Spirit be with you when you take another breath. We are not the center of God's world. On the spiritual path, there comes a point when we're not even the center of our own lives.

Several years ago, I attended a monthlong conference at the University of Toronto. Despite the fact that I had very little money, I really wanted to go. I applied for and received a scholarship that would cover tuition, but none of my living expenses. My desire and determination to participate in this conference were so strong that I ignored the painfully obvious "logistical" problems. I just went. It was that simple. Nothing was going to prevent me from going.

During the first week, I ate with the homeless at the YMCA. This might have worked out, but the distance from the college to the YMCA and back was much too far. I couldn't be present for meal-time at the YMCA and make my classes on time. After a few days, I gave up on that idea. Instead, I tried to manage on the finger sand-wiches provided for the conference participants at afternoon tea. It was a ridiculous situation, both comical and pathetic. And yet it was becoming very serious. I was desperately hungry. I looked emaciated and sick. I knew it, and my teachers knew it.

At the beginning of the second week, a much older classmate offered to buy me lunch. I jumped at the opportunity. Introductions were made rather quickly on the way to the restaurant, where we continued our heady discussion concerning the morning lecture. After a while, he politely asked about me and my studies. When I mentioned my interest in indigenous peoples and traditional forms of healing, he probed my intent with a questioning eye; but other-wise, he showed little obvious interest. Maybe halfway through our lunch, he expressed some polite concern about my sickly appearance.

He asked several discreet but fatherly questions about how I was doing; then, he said it would be his pleasure to help me stay well-fed during the remaining few weeks of the conference. Given my situation, I had no choice but to accept his offer, which I did with overwhelming gratitude.

A few days later, the organizer of the conference saw me talking with my new friend. Later in the afternoon, while we were both eating finger sandwiches, he asked if I realized who my friend really was. When I said no, he said, "This is a famous novelist," and he gave me his name. I was dumbfounded. We had only exchanged first names. I had admired this man's writing for nearly a decade. He was a devout Roman Catholic, a keen observer of contemporary spiritual life, and a great writer. That evening, I asked why he had not said anything about who he was. He sat quietly for a moment, and then asked whether it would have made a difference. All that mattered to him was that I was a sincere and honest person who needed some help. But as we talked more, I realized that he wanted me to understand something more: ordinary acts of loving-kindness reveal everything about life's meaning.

When the conference was over and I was back in my home, I had a series of perplexing and powerful dreams. Their meaning was completely beyond me, but I knew my soul had been deeply stirred by everything that had happened at the conference. It was then that I received a phone call from a close friend in Brazil. He was an anthropologist, living with an isolated tribe in the Amazon rain forest, and we hadn't spoken for several years. My friend said that he had traveled a full day to a nearby mission in order to use their telephone. The elder shaman in his village wanted him to give me a message, which was the reason he called. As it turned out, his message related to a crucial aspect of my dreams. My friend asked, "Does this make sense to you? Is it helpful?" I said, "Definitely yes." At that time, I had never been to Brazil and knew nothing about the shaman. The message isn't important for the purposes of this letter, but I will tell you that it helped me through an extremely difficult spiritual passage. That generous man may have saved my life, without my ever meeting him.

A devout Christian novelist and an indigenous shaman—two very different but wise people from vastly different cultures, with religious beliefs and perspectives on life that were worlds apart. They had virtually nothing in common, except for this: both of them followed their own spiritual paths, and they were both incredibly kind people. Neither of them wanted anything in return—nothing. Neither of them wanted to know about my beliefs, and neither of them wanted me to adopt theirs. Neither of them was concerned about defending "his beliefs" over and against another's. They were both firmly rooted in their own spiritual traditions. They both helped me understand that the spiritual path is not about "me," just as this story is not about me, nor about them. They both knew that the spiritual path is about God—and God is love. They had made the passage.

Faithfully yours.

29. LISTENING

My Dear Friend,

I have just returned from a long, relaxing visit with some people I've known nearly thirty years. We all stayed in a lovely and surprisingly affordable mountain inn, and spent a great deal of time doing very little. Most afternoons were given to solitary pursuits: reading, walking, resting. In the evenings, we gathered around the dinner table and talked, often late into the night. The whole time—being alone *and* with friends—was a blessing for which I am truly thankful.

Had it been possible, I would have gladly replied to you much sooner. As it turned out, your letter arrived shortly after I left; and it remained here, unopened at home, for nearly two weeks. Now, having read it several times, I am struck, yet again, by your exceptionally good instincts. I don't want to seem insensitive or abrupt, but you're right about the change in our relationship: a parting of sorts is taking place. The need for my counsel has passed, and the time has come for us to move ahead, each in our own way. Although I completely understand your apprehension, I must emphasize that this change is both necessary and good. I have great confidence in you; and I want you to know, with the same confidence in me, that you're neither losing a friend, nor being abandoned. Quite the opposite! *We are friends,* true soul friends, and when soul friends say farewell, it only appears they're going separate ways. The path itself—the Spirit—forms a bond between them strong enough to endure every hardship, not to mention distance. Follow the path long enough, and you'll know what I mean.

It is also true that continuing our relationship in its present form could do more harm than good. Even soul friends reach a point where the help we give *and* receive is no longer helpful. We have reached that point. At best, my letters could become a waste of your time and mine. Even worse, an unhealthy dependency could develop between us. This happens all too often, and the superbly preemptive protest in your letter tells me that this not only could happen, but it almost certainly would. If I continue writing in this way, you might follow the spiritual path vicariously through me, without taking the necessary steps on your own. You would be listening to me, rather than the one who called you to the spiritual path in the first place. I have no desire to assume that role, or to give the impression that I should or could.

Everything we've done so far, everything you've done, has been in preparation for this moment. Now, there is something you must do. To put it plainly, the time has come to return to the source of your call—to discover firsthand the reality, the Mystery, behind your awakening. And you must do this *within yourself*—that is to say, without substantial encouragement or interference from me. I realize how peculiar this seems. It should. The frantic, worried pace of our lives empties the most basic spiritual truths of their essential meaning. We want spirituality, for example, but we're too wrapped up with the way things are to take the Spirit very seriously. It's the same with praying—it can become an invitation to close rather than open our minds, and to avoid responding to injustices that require our help in the here and now. In fact, I am encouraging you to pray, but I mean a great deal more than this. As absurdly simple as it sounds, I'm asking you to live a prayerful life, in every respect, by learning to be a good listener. I'm quite serious about this. I hope you will make listening your spiritual practice. In fact, I would like to see your whole life oriented around listening. The purpose of my letter is to explain why this is so important.

Ultimately, I'm talking about "the God question," and I'm telling you how to find the kind of answer the spiritual path really offers. Trust me. It will be more than enough, more than you would ever dream. This will require patience, considerable commitment on your part, and, above all, faith. I'm asking you to listen as an act of faith. You could collect evidence for (and against) God's existence out in the world. I'll admit it seems like a reasonable thing to do, but it never takes us very far. The reason is not difficult to figure out. By assuming the role of judge—who would believe that we can decide these things—the "object" of our search recedes into the distance, present as an idea, but strangely out of reach, and therefore absent. But God is not an object, and the soul knows another, ancient, and more reliable route leading to a different kind of answer.

There is something—the Spirit—that is alive and well in the great body of life. To find this profound Mystery and experience it firsthand, we must learn to listen. The Spirit knows who we are and where we are better than we do. I know you still find this difficult to believe, and you will until you realize it within yourself. You can feel it happening already. It's the same in every tradition I know. What we first perceive as the call to awaken gradually becomes a claim that God makes on us. "You are mine," God says—it's not the other way around. We're not the center of the universe; we're not even the center of our own world; and it's God who is looking for evidence of love within us. We may avoid this claim on our lives. We may resist at every turn. Nonetheless, the claim is real; it calls out a response; and the response we make is the evidence we give.

We can only guess how God answers "the human question." We certainly run around a lot. We're busy. We talk incessantly to others and to ourselves, often about God, without listening nearly as much as we would like to believe. We tell ourselves that being "in the world, but not of it," as Jesus taught, means believing that we're right, while closing our ears, our eyes, and our minds to anything suggesting we might be wrong. It would be comic, if it weren't so horribly tragic. As the circle of know-it-all faith widens, the circle of listening shrinks. Yet we know, some part of us knows, that we're in deep trouble with each other, and in deeper trouble with Mother Earth and Father Sky. So, what's our response? We take as much as we can, as fast as we can, before the bottom falls out.

Apparently there's a close relationship between talking without listening, taking without giving, and avoiding the mere possibility that the Spirit might have something to say.

So, here's the real question: How is God answering "the human question" in you? I'm not going to tell you what to do; I wouldn't dream of saying "believe this" or "do that" and only good things will come your way; and I hope you will *not* make up your mind about "the God question," if that means believing you have all the answers. I'll say it again: my counsel is to orient your life around listening—as an act of faith. Don't misunderstand. I most definitely want you to speak. I want you to speak out about the issues of our day and whisper love songs with every truthful word you know. I want your actions to speak for you and well of you. And I hope you will speak from the same place within yourself that knows how to listen. Then, your words will be more than just talk. Listen like your life depends on it, but do not in any way, shape, or form believe everything you hear. There's a lot of nonsense out there— and within ourselves—which is all the more reason to listen more closely.

Think about it. Listening, rather than talking, allows us to occupy the space of our lives as free and sovereign people. Listening is the foundation of freedom; free expression is the outcome. If we love, we listen. If we really care about anyone or anything, we listen. If we want to make the world a better place, we listen. If we want to be free, if we want to find the source of our call, if we want to speak from a place that has any spiritual substance at all, then we must dedicate ourselves to listening every day, willingly and faithfully. Be a radical listener. Listen to your friends and enemies; listen to yourself; listen to the sunrise and to every living thing; and, above all else, listen to God, even when you think no one is there. People who spend a great deal of time praying know this. They become exceptionally good listeners. By experience, they've learned that listening, rather than talking, is the heart of prayer. They've realized that the purpose of the spiritual path is not to win friends for themselves, but to be a friend for the sake of others.

Let me tell a story about two teenage friends I know. They're both boys, about fourteen years old, and they're exceptionally good listeners. Do I hear you laughing? How can "good listener" and "teenager" possibly be spoken in the same breath? My experience is that when teenagers seem distracted and oblivious, they're usually paying attention in unexpected ways, and hearing nuances of meaning that we might completely overlook. Not long ago, when I drove into the parking lot of a small store near my house, I saw them sitting on the curb, talking. That's what I thought I saw. A few minutes later, I understood much better that they were sitting on the curb, talking *and* listening.

I was wrong about something else too. By their body language, I knew they recognized my car when I drove up; and because of the serious look on their faces, I assumed that my presence was unwelcome—that I would invade their privacy. I considered saying only hello before making my way inside the store. But, by the grace of God, I remembered that it was Friday afternoon and quickly asked about their plans for the weekend. To my surprise, they completely ignored my polite greeting and enlisted me in their otherwise private conversation. They wanted me there. They wanted me, as a friend, to bear witness to their lives.

This is what they said. They worked together, after school and on Saturdays, for a local craftsman and woodworker whom they admired immensely. He was their role model and mentor. He was teaching them a valuable skill, in which they found a great deal of satisfaction. The downside was that his business was small and struggling. Customers were often late paying their bills, so he was sometimes late with the payroll. This was the second consecutive Friday that they finished the workweek without being paid, and they were beginning to wonder whether they would ever see the money. Doubts were forming in their mind about their mentor-friend. Their frustration about this, combined with problems at school and home, plus the recent closing of some local companies, left them facing some grim questions: Can anyone really be trusted—employers, teachers, parents? Will our lives always be like this? If so, what's the point of trying? I should add that these same questions are asked just as much by their parents, and for the same reasons.

Having said all this, they asked me what I thought. First, I suggested that they have another talk with their employer, this time making it clear that they wanted to be fair-minded about him, but they expected to be treated fairly in return (a few days later they did exactly that, and they were paid soon thereafter). Next, I asked if they had ever heard of the spiritual path. Their reply being no, I said they were doing a good job following it anyway, and I was proud of them. Although I addressed the circumstances of their job first, from my point of view the real story was in *how* they told it—as you will momentarily understand.

The heart of my comments involved their openness to life, which was evident in the way they expressed themselves. They took turns, each talking and listening with dignity and respect. I especially liked how one of the boys asked the other to explain more fully what he meant. This simple request indicated genuine interest in his friend's experience. In other words, they cared about each other. Even more, it suggested that they had not made up their minds about God and the world, which often happens as we grow older. They were still asking questions, thinking for themselves, and remaining open to alternative possibilities. That is terribly important on the spiritual path. Disenchantment has a way of closing off the give-and-take of genuine, honest conversation. Yet they embodied the words they spoke by being present and available to each other, while their listening presence bore witness to the holy silence between the words they spoke. Those two teenagers would not have known it, but sitting on the curb in front of that store, they were much closer to the Holy Mystery than they ever would have imagined. They occupied the space of their lives, rather than being so preoccupied with their talking as to be somewhere else, or someone else, or no one. They were being true soul friends. I love those kids.

The sacred texts of all spiritual traditions are filled with experiences just like theirs and ours—the ego chill of feeling the rug pulled from under our feet, for reasons we neither like nor understand. We find ourselves sitting on a curb, talking on the phone, watching television, wherever—wondering what's going on, telling ourselves that no one can be trusted, and afraid that our lives might spin hopelessly out of control. Despite this, or because of it, a ray of hope is glimpsed within the confusion—which raises "the God question" in our minds. We can deny it, whether through sheer avoidance or, at the other extreme, by convincing ourselves that we've suddenly found all the answers. Or we can take another route. This, I'm glad to say, is what you have chosen to do. You were ambivalent, but curious enough to pursue the possibility, and open enough to seek the help of a trusted friend. Instead of closing your mind or losing it, you found your common sense. Now more than ever, you ask questions about life, without opposing faith to reason. You're involved with the community like few people I know. You've given your life a new structure by putting the brakes on personal spending—realizing that having more things will not make you more happy. The change I like best is that you take the time to listen to other people; and when you talk, you consider your words carefully and express yourself genuinely. All this tells me that you not only can follow the spiritual path, but you are following it.

If there is anything more I might say, anything that might be helpful, it involves the subtle and elusive meaning of "within yourself." "Solitude" is nearly the right word. It would be, except I'm not saying you need to be alone. Rilke had it right when he said, "We are solitary," whether we're alone or in the company of others, and he was writing to a friend! That is exactly my point: *We are friends* and *we are solitary*. In no way are these two thoughts contradictory. Everything I've said points directly to the place within ourselves where friendship and solitude meet. To find it, you must orient your whole life around listening, rather than talking. To be successful, you must practice listening every day, like your life depends on it. I can assure you that your efforts will not be wasted.

Listening is the foundation of prayerful living. Once we've established our lives there—within ourselves—listening and talking will come into their proper balance. Why is this important? The answer is simple. It creates the conditions for holy communion—being in the world, without being the center of our own. We become present to others and available to God. We can be a friend, rather than trying to win friends for ourselves. And when the opportune time finally arrives, when our minds have settled and our souls have the necessary desire, we will find what we're looking for. By our listening—as an act of faith, the Spirit will find us.

Faithfully yours.

30. Thankfulness

My Dear Friend,

You just never know how things are going to turn out. Only a short week ago, I thought I'd be writing a simple letter of farewell to a wonderful friend. That letter should have been easy. I knew what I wanted to say; but as much as I tried, I made no headway in actually saying it. At first, I thought a mild but annoying psychosomatic block might be at work—that is, I couldn't write that letter because I didn't want to say good-bye. It seemed reasonable, yet somehow I knew that wasn't the problem. After a few more unsuccessful attempts, I began to suspect some unfinished business, perhaps an unrealized *something* I needed to work through, which was more likely. The problem was that I had no inkling of what the problem might be.

Then, two seemingly unrelated events broke the ice. The first was the arrival of your note. I deeply appreciate the kind and thoughtful words, but I must say that your generosity goes too far. I fear that a pedestal may be forming in your mind, with me on it. On occasion, we all create idealized images of people who help us through rough times, like priests and therapists. Despite our good intentions, those images distort the truth about life and I would advise against them. I don't believe this is a serious issue between us, but it could become one. I'm talking about me as much as you—I might be tempted to believe whatever the pedestal implies. So, I welcome your kindness with an open heart, but for your sake and mine, let's keep our feet planted firmly on the ground.

Quite honestly, I might not have said anything about this or given it much thought had not the second event occurred so soon after your note arrived—within a half hour or less. I was sitting in the living room when an unusual wind blew across the mountains and through my yard. It took some time to understand its full meaning, but the wind helped me do what I could not accomplish on my own. Although my letter explains this in some detail, for now I'll only say that the wind—the Spirit—knocked that pedestal from under my feet in the very moment I was tempted to accept it. In doing so, I remembered something that's better not forgotten—namely, thankfulness. That, my friend, was my unfinished business, the unrealized something I needed to work through and tell you about. You'd think we would never forget anything so important and so basic, but we do; and as much as I hate to admit this, I did forget. So before saying farewell, I must tell this one last story, from beginning to end—a story about a letter that was never meant to be and a lesson in gratitude.

Let me begin by setting the record straight about the pedestal. Your exceptionally thoughtful note mentions my ardent love for nature, and especially my love for trees. Your impression of me is essentially right in that regard. My love for nature and trees is entirely genuine, deeply felt, and true in every respect except one—I absolutely loathe raking leaves. This sounds trivial and probably silly to you, but it's important to me. Just read my story before making a judgment. These small, seemingly insignificant facts about our lives can reveal a great deal about who we are. Even more, the Spirit of God works through them in unexpected ways. But I'm getting ahead of myself. I can't fully explain my dislike for raking. All I know is that when the beautiful yellow, orange, and red leaves of autumn begin to fall, my outlook on life takes a dramatic turn. Leaves on their branches are beautiful. Their colors reveal the glory of God. When they're on the ground, an awful dread fills my heart. This has been true ever since I was a child. It made me feel guilty then, and it still does.

Not much has changed between raking and me through the years, at least not until the last few days. When late September comes, I watch one unmerciful leaf after another pile up in my yard. I'm talking about an ungodly amount of leaves, nearly a foot or more in some places. I cope with it in much the same way that I deal with difficult people—by formulating a strategy. Basically, I map out a plan; reflect on it a few days, hoping to find the necessary resolve and good humor; and then I put my plan into action. It involves raking a little here and there every day, sometimes in the front of the house, other times in the back or on the sides. I realize it's a pitiful excuse for a strategy. Whether it makes my emotional burden any lighter or actual raking any easier are questions I don't care to answer. I pretend that it works, and that helps. But I can say with confidence that if I wait, it takes a week or more to complete my work, and that seems like a terribly long time.

This year has been different. I've been too busy to glance at the leaves, and I've had no time to strategize. This has magnified my dread to the point of making me want to scream or hide in the corner. All this changed when your note, and that unusual wind, arrived at my house. It was late in the afternoon. Like I said, I was sitting in the living room, thinking about your kind words. I heard a noise outside, and turned to look out the front window. The wind arrived suddenly from the west. This was no mere gust, but a sizable storm, strong enough to make the house shake. Was I worried about the house? No, but I should have been. As soon as I heard that sound, I knew what it might mean. At first, I laughed with giddy disbelief, and then I let loose with a display of joy resembling a cheerleader on the sidelines of a championship game. It was embarrassing, even to me.

Because the wind blew well into the night, I had to set my anticipation aside and get some sleep. It was early the next morning when I finally went outside. I couldn't believe it. No leaves could be found—not in the front of the house, not in the back, not anywhere in the yard. Oddly, the usual guilt I feel about my dislike for raking was replaced by guilt about not having to rake. I questioned whether I might've evaded my responsibility unfairly. What did I do? I went looking for the leaves. Can you believe it? I actually walked to my neighbor's house, thinking that if I found the leaves there, my duty would be to help them with their raking. It was a peculiar feeling, and I found myself asking some strange questions: If there were leaves in their yard, how would I know they were "mine"? And if they had been "mine," shouldn't they now be "theirs"? It didn't matter—there were no leaves. I felt like one of the disciples at the empty tomb. Jesus must have risen, because I was free. I didn't quite believe it, but the evidence could not be denied.

The story could have ended there. It would have, but the wind did more than blow away the leaves. It unearthed some old memories within me. I remembered my struggle with the leaves in childhood, and the suspiciously busy life I led even then. Care of the yard was my responsibility; and like all teenagers, I had places to go and people to see. In those days, I often played basketball after school or I went to the library. I loved doing both. I can't say I studied much; but I loved to read, so I made reasonably good grades. I lived for basketball. But something else was going on in my head too. Those after-school activities gave me the perfect excuse to avoid raking. In effect, I had a note to my parents from the principal that said:

Your son has important duties at school in the afternoons. Unfortunately, he will be unable to rake leaves. Please understand how important these activities are for him. By participating in team sports, he learns valuable lessons in healthy competition and cooperation; and of course, success in his studies is important for his future career—not to mention his happiness as a well-adjusted person who contributes to society in positive ways.

Although the note is make-believe, it accurately portrays the strategy I sometimes employed in my younger days. The reasoning behind it seemed legitimate; and in a very real sense, it was. I usually raked leaves on Saturdays, but the rest of the week was filled with other duties. This was accepted by nearly everyone—the school, my parents, and my friends—which made it seem official and morally right, almost. Classes ended around 3:00 P.M.; basketball practice began promptly at 4:00; and no team member in good standing could be late, or leave early. That was the rule. My parents encouraged me in this direction, and they were obligated to do so. Yet, in the back of my mind, I always knew how convenient it was for me. I was quite happy to avoid the responsibility that was clearly mine, and I don't recall even once suggesting that I might miss practice now and again to fulfill it.

The wind also stirred up another, more important memory. Until I reached driving age, my dad picked me up at the gym after basketball practice. On our way home one evening, when he turned into the driveway, we both noticed our beautiful, freshly raked yard. I sat there, quietly, in the passenger seat. I don't know whether the car actually stopped, but time, as I experienced it, certainly did. Some kind of response was required from me, so I asked the inevitable question, "Who raked the yard?" With a clear, matter-of-fact voice, he said, "Your mother." I knew the answer already. He knew that I knew, and I knew that he knew. It didn't matter. The answer had to be given, just as the question had to be asked. I could feel the redness rising in my face. I looked at my dad; he looked at me, and then he said, "It's okay . . . just be sure to thank her." We got out of the car. I opened the door to the house, and did exactly as he encouraged me to do.

That happened nearly forty years ago. As soon as I remembered saying thank you to my mom, I realized the nature of my unfinished business today, and I knew how all this was connected: my inability to write the first letter, the arrival of your note, the wind sweeping away the leaves in my yard. I let myself believe that our work was complete, when it wasn't. Why? Because there were some issues around thankfulness that I need to work through. Never mind that I thought I only needed to say farewell. I was wrong about that. Never mind that I was busy. I've always been busy. In the moment of remembering, I was thankful for everything—for being alive, for life itself—and thankful to God for giving me the opportunity to be thankful.

And I laughed from the deepest part of my belly, mainly at myself. Laughter seemed totally appropriate in response to the playful, unpredictable, trickster-like quality of the whole series of events, which I interpreted as a sign of the Spirit's presence. This is a

subtle and important point I'm making, and easily misunderstood—
the Spirit can be unimaginably playful. A lot of people don't believe
that, but I know it's true. I'm not saying the love of God is capricious
or unreliable in any way. We're the ones who play games with God's
love—trying to pin down the Spirit, deciding where the Spirit can
and cannot be, fighting about the Spirit's gender, and so on. There
are always issues of discernment involved, but the Spirit comes and
goes where it will—like the wind—just as Jesus said.

I think we've turned reality around. We cast ourselves in the
Spirit's role by calling ourselves free and righteous, but we're really
maneuvering for control. It makes me wonder what Jesus intended
when he said he would send the Spirit as our Counselor and Advocate.
I believe him, but I doubt he meant that we only need to carve out
some space now and again in our busy lives so we might receive the
Spirit's help. On the other hand, I suppose it's better than nothing.

My experience in the last few days turned the tables on me and raised
a question that is funny and terribly serious at the same time: Have I
understood that the Spirit is not a supporting character in a story about
me, while someone else rakes the leaves? It goes without saying that
we should be thankful for all the things people do for us. The issue is
whether we've learned to accept the responsibilities that we would like
to avoid, and to be thankful while fulfilling them. And I'm talking about
a great deal more than raking. Who will rebuild our broken communities? Feed the hungry? Clean up the water we drink and the air we
breathe? For God's sake, in most of the world who will carry the water?
Who will do all these things, if not us? Are we waiting for our mothers
or Jesus to come to the rescue, while we're busy with other things—
telling our own stories? The writer of Ecclesiastes looked at all our
deeds and famously described them as "vanity and a chasing after wind"

(Ecclesiastes 1:14, NRSV). What do we think he meant? That the lessons of the wind are a waste of time? Or that chasing a story about ourselves is a waste of our lives? End-times are like that. Stories about ourselves come to an end. When the pedestals fall, an awakening begins.

Only a week ago, I was struggling with a letter I couldn't write. Today, I'm thankful that I didn't set down some words that seemed empty and incomplete. A great deal has happened since then, and now I can say it—farewell, my dear friend—because I've found the end of my story. It hasn't ended yet, but I'm beginning to see it. I caught a glimpse of it this morning, when I saw some leaves falling in the front yard. It was inevitable that this would happen. Yet for the first time I saw them in a different way. I saw my life in them, and theirs in mine. Instead of dread, there was a smile and a laugh, and I understood that our final destination arrives sooner than we want to believe. We don't think about it much when we're younger. Then, we have places to go, people to see, and dreams of a different kind. Of course, I'm as busy today as I've ever been, and I dream of the people I love and care for, the rivers, and the trees. I realize, better than before, that remembering the past is another form of dreaming. I see myself in the leaves, and I know the moment will someday come when the wind—the Spirit—carries me home. This seems like a dream too, but I know it's real.

Today, I think I might actually enjoy the feel of a rake in my hands. Yes, I'm going to do exactly that. I'm going to feel the cool breeze blowing against my face; I'm going to laugh some more; and I'm going to be thankful. Life really is a series of moments. Every moment pours out the love of God. You and the wind helped me remember this. I cannot thank you enough.

Faithfully yours.

AUTHOR'S NOTE

The kindness of many remarkable friends brought this book into the light of day. I've written it with them in mind, and I have no idea how to acknowledge this or to express my gratitude enough. They come from so many walks of life: accountants, anthropologists, artists, astronomers, builders, carpenters, civil servants, community organizers, disc jockeys, doctors, ecologists, gardeners, healers, librarians, mechanics, mothers and fathers, plumbers, politicians, priests, prisoners, prison guards, reporters, secretaries, shamans, shopkeepers, social workers, teachers, and stonemasons. There are more. Despite the wildly different opinions they may have about this book, they've all played a part in its realization. They did this simply by being who they are. Some may be surprised that I would think of them here, but it's probably good that we don't always perceive or understand the profound influence we can have on our friends. Others will detect their presence in these pages yet prefer to remain anonymous. I can understand that. I've taken great care to honor their wishes and to protect still others who might not have given it much thought.

I want to mention a few by name: Fred Barber, Joan Brady, Peter Bridgford, Jim Carpenter, Cyclone Covey, Laura Day, Jim Fenhagen, Judith Gillette, Margaret Guenther, James Hillman, Emmett Jarrett, John and Elisabeth Koening, John Luce, Oren Lyons, Madeline Mathiot, Jim and Pamela Morton, Paul and Beverly Reeves, Terry Rogers, Sheila Siragusa, Mark Sisk, Dave Sparrow, Masud Ibn Syedullah, Pundit Ragmani Tiganit, Carol Tookey, and Swami Ved. A special thanks is reserved for Emma Cook, Madeleine L'Engle, Paul Moore, Darrell Posey, and Davey Zehmer. Their souls have passed beyond this world, and they are greatly missed. All these people have contributed enormously to my life and to this book. The same can be said for whole groups of people and institutions: St. John's Episcopal Church (Ellenville, New York), the Third Order of the Society of Saint Francis, the Community of the Holy Spirit, Little Portion Friary, Holy Cross Monastery, the Office of the Anglican Observer at the United Nations, the General Theological Seminary, the Iona Community (Scotland), the Himalayan Institute, Wake Forest University, Louisiana State University in Baton Rouge, the Department of Anthropology at the State University of New York in Buffalo, the Cathedral of St. John the Divine (Manhattan), St. John's Grace Episcopal Church (Buffalo), the Trinity Grants Program, the people of Ronda and Elkin, North Carolina, and all my neighbors on Bee Hive Road.

I've been enormously dependent on the goodwill, professional skill, and friendship of Susan Petersen Kennedy, Joel Fotinos, and Sarah Litt of Jeremy P. Tarcher/Penguin, and Elizabeth Bortka, my meticulous copy editor. Susan's thoughtful, persistent encouragement during the earliest stages of the book made it happen. She suggested that I write in the form of letters, and I'm glad she did.

Joel and Sarah were remarkably adept at drawing out what I really wanted to say, which was no small task. After waiting patiently while I recovered from surgery, they provided the assistance I needed at the right time and in just the right measure. Then, as it turned out, they waited some more, way beyond the call of duty, for which I am truly thankful. The opportunity to work with them has been my immense pleasure and good fortune. Of course, any errors that remain are my responsibility alone.

My parents, Bob and Sally, my sister, Wendy, and her husband, Joe Worrell, all have a great sense of humor. Even a small laugh now and then goes a long way in this day and age, and they have a never-ending supply. My wife, Asha, has the patience of a saint, and, for other reasons too, she is wise beyond her years. Without her loving support, I would have had neither the time nor the peace of mind to write even one page. I owe them the world.

Jeff Golliher

2008

ABOUT THE AUTHOR

The Reverend Jeffrey Mark Golliher, Ph.D., a cultural anthropologist and priest in the Episcopal Church, has traveled widely to understand the spiritual dimension of the environmental crisis. For more than ten years, he was canon for Environmental Justice and Community Development at the Cathedral of St. John the Divine in Manhattan. Today, he is a parish priest and spiritual director, working with people who want to live in more spiritually aware, healthy, and sustainable ways. As the environmental representative for the worldwide Anglican Communion at the United Nations, he has organized global conferences on spirituality, ecology, and community development, and he has written and edited numerous books and articles on these subjects for the church and the United Nations. He was born and raised in the Blue Ridge Mountains of western North Carolina. Currently, he lives with his wife, Asha, in Upstate New York.